BLAZE YOUR OWN TRAIL

Twenty Leaders in Commercial Real Estate
Share Their Unique Paths to Success

by

Pamela J. Goodwin

Featured Authors:

Patty Bender

Holland Burton

Lynn Dowdle

Jennifer Frank

Pamela J. Goodwin

Sharon Herrin

Danielle Kaufman

Leslie J. Mayer

Heather McClure

Mollie Mossman

Amy Pjetrovic

Heather Prichard

Kara Rafferty

Tanya Ragan

Valerie Richardson

Alice Seale

Karla Smith

Jan (Cycon) True

Lynn Van Amburgh

Lisa Walker

DEDICATION – THANK YOU

Thank you to all the authors who took time to share their total of 597 years of knowledge and experience being in the commercial real estate industry.

Thank you for reading this collection of questions and answers from the top female leaders in the industry. May you take the information and blaze your own trail!

Table of Contents

PATTY BENDER

Company: Vista Private Equity

Years in Commercial Real Estate: 41

How did you get started in commercial real estate and what age?

I moved to Houston (from PA) when I was 26 and became a Fashion Buyer at Foley's Department stores. One of my strongest relationships there, the assistant Director of Human Resources, became a good friend. She left Foley's to become the Human Resource Director for a public Real Estate Investment Trust (REIT), Weingarten Realty. She later convinced me at the age of 29 to join Weingarten as a Property Manager and I remained at the company for 34 years, eventually leading the company's sales and marketing teams.

Do you have an industry specialty or niche?

My niche is management, management consulting, streamlining leasing processes, lease negotiations, training salespeople and new development.

What advice do you have for someone entering the commercial real estate industry?

Find a company that will offer some training - either a mentor who will take the time to teach or possibly a seasoned company with a training program. Also, self-awareness is key as this is a conversational/people-oriented business. Lastly, it is important to find a company that has a cultural fit as we spend more time with our work family than we do with our own!

Did/do you have a mentor and how did you find him or her?

During my 34 years in the public REIT, I had a mentor who was also somewhat of a father figure. His name was Martin Debrovner and he served as co-chairman of the Weingarten Realty. He was one of the best sounding boards I have ever had and cared about my growth in leadership and management. Martin offered wise counsel on both deal making matters and personnel issues. He passed away a few years ago and I miss him!

What is the best advice you have received?

To raise my level of discomfort and charge forward - doing something that causes me to feel uncomfortable. For me, this was moving from property management to sales/leasing at 31 years old. HA! I never looked back. Thank you, Mike Wood, the man who pushed me and was a great supervisor.

What are three skills you need to be in the industry?

The ability to negotiate, network and solid people skills; the ability to understand legal documents, pro-formas and financials; and the ability to multi-task.

What failure stands out for you and what did you learn?

My failure was my attempt to lease an anchor space to Crate & Barrel in the River Oaks Shopping Center in Houston; I was competing with the Houston based Highland Village Center. I spent weeks with our market research team building my case for our location and during that time became very close with the Crate & Barrel team. I learned the value of the team approach to dealmaking including construction, market research and marketing in the process. We lost the deal to Highland Village and they are still there today but losing was a win because I became a more well-rounded and seasoned leasing executive.

What are the steps you have taken to succeed in commercial real estate?

I have taken many steps. The most rewarding was graduating with my MBA at the age of 40; the education taught me about critical thinking and I also became better at the financial side of our business. Another critical step was to become a lead volunteer with ICSC. I directed the Texas convention in the early 2000's and not only improved my public speaking but also make some lifelong business friends. A third step is to simply never stop networking, whether it be a Bisnow event, a Crew luncheon or a Deals In Heels event.

What question are you asked the most?

I am often asked how I became a leader of a public REIT managing more than 100 employees across 26 states and 13 offices. I always answer – "little by little." Starting in property management and then leasing provided such a well-rounded background to grow in the business. I truly believe the problem-solving skills I learned in property management helped me to become a more successful manager later on in life.

What are the greatest challenges you have faced in the industry?

The challenge for the 2008 recession. At that time, I was managing the leasing team and as Director of Leasing, was asked to do whatever I could to maintain 90% or higher occupancy across the national portfolio. To accomplish this, my legal team and I developed the RAPID LEASE, an eight-page document that required no negotiation. This lease was utilized in the field during the recession and offered the opportunity for a start-up to sign a short and simple lease. It worked like magic and our occupancy never fell below 90% and my leasing agents could close deals and provide for their families.

What is the best negotiation tip you have learned?

SILENCE - let the other party go first and let there be silence as it makes everyone uncomfortable but at the same time, thoughtful.

What time management tools or skills do you use?

I manage my time via my electronic calendar and a list on my desk. There is nothing better that checking something off the list!

What advice would you give to the next generation of female leaders?

There is simply no glass ceiling. Women are better listeners, they embrace empathy and humility at a higher level than most males, which gives them an edge in career building and negotiations. Continue to develop the skills that create a true culture of success and capability. Also, put yourself out there by speaking in public or volunteering for a presentation. True leaders lead.

What organizations or groups do you recommend becoming part of your network?

After securing a real estate license, I would also recommend a broker's license which has benefited me in personal transactions over the years. In addition, I highly recommend Commercial Real Estate Women (CREW), Urban Land Institute (ULI) and ICSC and attending networking functions such as Bisnow.

For me, continuing my education helped me grow. In property management, I attained my Certified Property Manager (CPM) through Institute of Real Estate Management (IREM) and later graduated with an MBA which supported my critical thinking and leadership.

Looking back, what is one thing you wish you knew at the beginning of your career?

How much I was going to love it! I probably would have skipped the three years at Foley's and moved right into commercial real estate. Also, I wish I would have taken more financial courses in college; the more one understands the financial picture, the easier it is to negotiate and add value.

BIO - PATTY BENDER

Patty Bender is a partner at Vista Private Equity, a regional shopping center developer with forty (40) years of history in the Texas markets. She is currently developing a service -oriented shopping center in McKinney, TX, and is expanding Vista's footprint in the DFW market. Also, Ms. Bender owns a consulting services business (Circle Real Estate Partners) and has advised real estate firms in the hospitality, retail and commercial sectors. Her expertise includes marketing and branding, development and land planning, tenant mix, lease negotiations and workouts, sales team management and associated processes.

Ms. Bender served as an Executive Vice President with Weingarten Realty Investors, enjoying a successful leadership career with this national REIT, traded on the New York stock exchange. During her (33) thirty-three-year tenure, she directed the Leasing, Marketing and Market Research departments. Ms. Bender was responsible for the net income of 400 shopping centers and directed all transactions in existing assets, re-developments and new developments. Her team's responsibilities included anchor and shop tenant replacement, re-merchandising, and repositioning assets to maximize cash flow. In addition, her team directed the company's brand positioning, corporate marketing, public relations, social media programs and web site development.

Ms. Bender was particularly focused on the design and development of the open-air lifestyle centers owned by Weingarten Realty. She also was involved in the design and leasing of several mixed-use project on the west coast.

During Ms. Bender's tenure at Weingarten, she developed and implemented training programs for the sales team. Each training course was developed by Ms. Bender and covered topics such as Sales Motivation, Leadership & Team Management, Cold Calling Methodology, Customer Development, Retail Strategies and Market Analysis.

Prior to joining the company, Ms. Bender was a Senior Fashion Buyer at Foley's Department Store. This experience served to enhance her understanding of the shopping center business from a retail perspective.

Ms. Bender holds a Master of Business Administration with a concentration in Marketing/Management from the University of St. Thomas and a Bachelor of Science Degree from Westchester University. She is a National Association of Corporate Directors (NACD) "Fellow"; also, she holds a Texas Real Estate Broker's License, a Certified Property Manager Designation (CPM), and is an active member of the International Council of Shopping Centers.

In 2009, Rice University asked Ms. Bender to develop a Real Estate course for the Jones School of Business. Since that time, she served six years as an Adjunct Professor teaching her course entitled "Marketing Based Project Analysis."

In 2011, she was asked to join the Francesca's Collection Board of Directors, where she serves on both the Compensation and the Nominating & Corporate Governance committees. In addition, she served on the Board of Uptown Houston for 20 years, chairing the Uptown Marketing Committee, and currently serves on the Board of North Texas Leukemia & Lymphoma Society.

Patty Bender

pbender@vistagroupllp.com

Vista Properties

1127 Eldridge Parkway

Houston, TX 77077

713 299 1828 cell

HOLLAND BURTON

Company: Propelled Brands

Years in Commercial Real Estate: 39

How did you get started in commercial real estate and what age?

My path into the world of corporate real estate was very atypical. I earned a B.A. in French (University of North Carolina at Chapel Hill), and I went on to earn a Master of International Management (American Graduate School of International Management, now Thunderbird School of Global Management), as I felt that adding a business degree was a more practical way to possibly use my language degree in a career. While still in graduate school, I interviewed with Popeyes Fried Chicken; the company made me an offer and I started in their Real Estate Department directly out of grad school. This was a significant first step for me in setting my career path in real estate. The person who hired me believed that an individual who understood international business could go into markets and understand what people do, where they go and why; this is essentially what all real estate professionals do on a daily basis. I was just 23 when I went to work for Popeyes Fried Chicken and the company was still headquartered in New Orleans, LA.

My position was a Development Intelligence Analyst in the company's Real Estate Department, and I did on-site market research for the company to create franchise territories for new Franchisees. After visiting any market which had franchise interest or activity, I prepared Market Development Plan reports that the Real Estate Managers would then use to assist the Franchisees in finding their new locations. The plans were created using demographics, competitive maps, and competitive market information that I obtained during my trips to each market. There was very little information available without visiting the market when I began my career. I often met with city officials and Chambers of Commerce to find out about the growth areas of the cities I visited. I used the yellow pages to find competitors and paper maps with colored dots to create market maps for Franchisees. These maps would help everyone understand the key activity corridors in each market and the trade areas which were the most critical to a franchisee's success.

I drove endlessly and used a small tape recorder to make sure I could preserve all my data gathering before I left a given market. This was before cell phones, web-based searches, on-line demographics programs and Google Earth. So, driving the market and making notes via tape recorder was the most efficient way to ensure that you had all the information that you needed within a reasonable time. When I ordered demographics, it would often take over a week to receive them via USPS; an expedited order was to receive the demographics in less than five days via fax. If you needed an aerial photograph of a market, you might have to contact a pilot to fly over the trade area and take the photo for you. Today, all these activities can be done more or less with the touch of a button and the information that you require for real estate development planning is instantly available. But I am extremely thankful that I had the experience of driving all over America (and Canada and a few other interesting places) in order to understand market dynamics. I always try to go drive a market, even today, after doing my web-based research. Nothing replaces seeing how consumers move in the trade area and how active (or inactive) a trade area actually is.

From this research-based beginning, I moved into a Real Estate Manager position. Over time, I have held multiple positions with multiple companies all with different titles (Director, Senior Director, Vice President), but in all these positions, I believe that my background in the market-based research has been the foundation to my success.

Do you have an industry specialty or niche?

Personally, my feeling is that my specialty is in small shop retail leasing for corporations. I have operated within this framework for approximately 80% of my career. In addition, I have worked for numerous bakeries, bakery café and coffee concepts, so I would consider that another niche for myself as I understand a great deal about these concepts and what site characteristics such companies consider essential for their success. Finally, most of the companies that I have worked for have also been in the business of franchising. Understanding how to conduct the business of real estate within a franchise system is another area of expertise for me.

What advice do you have for someone entering the commercial real estate industry?

For someone entering the commercial real estate industry through a corporate real estate position, it is important to realize that this is a unique position, offering an opportunity to engage and learn about many different aspects of a company. To negotiate a great real estate deal for a company, you need to really understand the concept that you represent.

Spend time with the Marketing Team and learn about your target customer as this will affect the demographics that you evaluate. Spend time with the Finance and/or Accounting Teams in order to understand the concept's profit and loss statement (P & L); knowing about the store level economics such as labor costs, product costs, required services and the investment cost of the build-out, fixtures and equipment will help you in understanding the maximum occupancy rate a new location can absorb and the sales required to be profitable. Spend time with the Operations Team to understand any special concerns they have based upon other locations that are operating and challenges they have faced with parking, patios, less complimentary co-tenants, and other issues. Finally, spend time with the Legal Team to understand how to best negotiate a letter of intent and a lease so that the site is set up for success from the beginning.

Understand who your competitors are and study their approach to locations as well as your company's approach. You want to understand the sales mix for your concept and how that might impact the type of real estate you pursue. A breakfast-oriented concept may need to be on the going to work side of the road. A lunch-oriented concept may need to be near a concentration of offices and not in a suburb. A dinner or special occasion concept may need to be in an entertainment setting.

A snack concept will need easy access and convenience at various times of the day (and may be better suited to non-traditional real estate such as an airport). A service-oriented concept may have less need to be at "main and main," and may be focused on other issues like a lower rent.

I also recommend learning as much as possible about all the different aspects of the industry by not creating a niche for yourself in your early career. Let your "niche" evolve over time after you have experience in many different areas. With time and experience, you are able to choose the types of projects which you are most passionate about.

Depending upon whether you are a real estate broker or in a corporate real estate position, this may mean different things. For a real estate broker, it may mean learning about retail leasing, industrial leasing, and office leasing as well as about development projects and/or investment properties. Some brokers focus only on Tenant Rep while others focus on Landlord representation. Other boutique firms may specialize in franchise development or in being an outsourced real estate department for smaller retailers.

For a corporate real estate position, it may be learning about different types of retail development. Retail and restaurant concepts develop in free-standing, single tenant buildings, in small shop space, in malls and in airports, inside of other stores (such as a national coffee shop inside of a grocery store or a department store) or in other facilities (universities, libraries, etc.). Some companies only lease their properties, others prefer a ground lease, while others will prefer to purchase their properties for development. Different types of retail have different needs; a quick-serve restaurant will want a drive-thru lane while a full-service restaurant needs more parking than just about any other use. Post-pandemic, almost every retail and restaurant concept want to have spaces for pick-up and a patio. Conversely, service-oriented retailers may have low parking requirements. Each of these different types of real estate requires different negotiating strategies. Learning about many different types of uses and the way they choose locations is interesting and useful, no matter whether you are on the corporate side or the brokerage side of the business.

As you consider job opportunities, think about the type of real estate that the company pursues and whether you are passionate about it. If you do not have much experience yet, try to work for different companies and learn about the different types of development. Eventually, your path will become clear to you.

Did/do you have a mentor and how did you find him or her?

I believe that I have had many mentors throughout my career, but they were informal. Frequently, I have worked for them directly and have learned valuable career lessons from their leadership skills. In other cases, I have had mentors by having the ability to spend time with others in executive level leadership either at my company or through industry associations or events. Most of these "mentors" were informal relationships and the individuals may not have even realized that I considered them mentors.

I have only had one "official" mentorship during my career and that was with a group in Atlanta which was called The Georgia 100 (now Women Who Win). This is a women's mentorship program for women leaders in all types of business. I was very lucky in joining this group as my official "Mentor" was a Life Coach by profession. She provided me with fantastic tools and information on leadership that were based in psychology and understanding others' wants and needs. I still use some of the lessons I learned through this relationship to this day. I would like to mention that I was nominated to it by a Senior Vice President who I considered one of my "unofficial" mentors – she obviously also had a major impact on my professional life.

What is the best advice you have received?

Early in my real estate career, someone told me that the worst thing you can hear on a first offer is "I accept." This has only happened to me one time within my career, but I have never forgotten it. About 25 years ago, I was negotiating a small space with a mall landlord; I thought I had made an extremely aggressive offer, but it was accepted with virtually no pushback or changes from the landlord (very unusual in a mall negotiation at the time!). Even though I had negotiated a great deal and the company went on to have a very profitable store in this location, I knew in that instance that I had left money on the table. It always bothered me, and I still remember it to this day.

What are three skills you need to be in the industry?

Curiosity, resilience, and a good networking system. It is very important to be prepared in real estate as you are always gathering information that you might use to make a case for (or against) a location. Preparedness is rooted in curiosity. In order to be prepared, you really need to explore a trade area, ask questions about it of other tenants, other landlords, other professionals and people who live in the area. Drive by at different times of the day to gain different perspectives on how a location might perform. If you are not curious, you may not go the extra mile and find the growing, alternative trade area nearby…or the competitor who is new to the market and has already located in this new trade area with their first location. Read the news about what is trending, monitor social media, attend industry events to learn about new developments and new concepts, and finally, pay attention to what you see happening in the market. In other words, just be curious and you will be surprised how much this helps you be successful.

It is also important to be resilient. A career in real estate is one in which you may be told "no" on a frequent basis. This is not a personal insult. It just means that the opportunity you presented was not right at that time for that company (or your concept was not a good fit for a certain project). Keep researching and paying attention to what the company indicates that it wants from growth as well as how the market is changing and eventually the right opportunity will present itself. A win is even more satisfying when you've been told "no" and you find another way to address the need successfully.

Finally, a good networking system is extremely helpful. People move around frequently in today's economy. They change companies, they move to different states, they may even change their area of expertise. As your former colleagues and associates expand their knowledge base through these experiences, the sharing of information with you will help you to expand your knowledge base as well. Although it is sometimes difficult to find time to do your daily work <u>and</u> keep in touch with others outside of your company, it is key in today's world where the sharing of information can be critical to success. Take time to nurture your network.

What failure stands out for you and what did you learn?

A failure that stands out to me is one that I think about quite frequently because it happened in a trade area that I shop in often. A few years ago, I presented an opportunity to the company I worked for at the time in a fast-growing suburb of the Dallas-Ft. Worth market.

Costco was already under construction in this trade area and the residential growth in this market was off the charts. The site was near a major employer, a major hospital, and was on a commuting corridor to a major highway. Several other well-known retailers were coming in as generators at this shopping center as well.

I negotiated a letter of intent for a small shop space in a strip center which would be on an outparcel in front of Costco. This deal had it all: reasonable rent, tenant improvement allowance, a full Landlord work letter, a drive-thru lane and a patio. It literally felt like it was one of the best deals I had ever negotiated. Better yet, the Landlord was someone who I had worked with on a deal for another company and, because that deal was so successful, he wanted to work with me again and with any company that I represented.

Despite all these positives, I did not secure Real Estate Committee approval on this site. It was decided that we should go closer to the highway where there was a more established shopping center, even though there was a competitor at that shopping center which prohibited our use (which meant it was highly unlikely we would ever develop in this trade area). Fast forward five to six years and there are many competitors in this fast casual category located at the Costco shopping center or across from it. Clearly, all of the competition was able to see the potential of this trade area. For some reason, I was unable to communicate the potential of this trade area to my company and they passed on a great opportunity.

Because I shop in this trade area, this is probably the failure that I think about the most. In retrospect, I have realized the company did not actually want to commit to growth through new locations; their preference was to re-engineer the menu and to remodel existing locations. Their goal was really to grow by driving profitability through existing locations, not through expansion. What I learned is that by pushing growth through expansion, I was not really aligned with the company's goals, and I turned my attention to renewals.

Working on renewal agreements which were structured to provide Tenant Improvement funds for the remodeling of existing highly profitable locations was much more enthusiastically embraced than new growth opportunities.

What are the steps you have taken to succeed in commercial real estate?

I believe I have already shared many of the steps that I have taken to be successful in commercial real estate. One additional recommendation that I have is to try to answer unsolicited phone calls and emails. It is harder in today's world because with technology, you may feel constantly bombarded by someone who believes that they have the perfect site or service for your company. Still, I have found this is a secret to success over time. I have had sites presented to me that were very desirable, simply because the leasing agent remembered that I always took their calls when they had very undesirable sites in the past, and I tried to be polite about those sites not being a good fit for my company.

Because of the courtesy I showed them, they remembered me when they did have a great opportunity. It's a reminder that this is a small world, and it can be a very small industry. I have also had service vendors for which I didn't have budget approval for at the time, but I found their service interesting; later, I have been able to circle back and engage when at another company which needed that service. In brief, the individual that you really do not have time for today may be extremely important to you in the future.

I have also embraced learning about aspects of development that support success in real estate, such as design and construction. Every real estate deal must eventually have a layout and it must be built. Most letters of intent and leases will have detailed design requirements and construction requirements. Learning more about these areas, even if you are not an expert, will make you a more valuable real estate executive.

What question are you asked the most?

The questions I am asked the most in my professional life have very little direct correlation with my real estate career. First, I am asked about my name (short answer: it is a family name). In some ways, having an unusual first name has been an unexpected benefit in this industry. Many people remember me because it is an unusual name.

Secondly, I am often asked about the "glamorous" life of traveling for business. Most people think traveling for business is very exciting and thrilling. And there are times that it is exciting. I have been to a majority of states and learned so much about so many major cities as well as very small towns across the country. I have spent time on site tours in Canada, Guam, and the Virgin Islands. I have been privy to some memorable experiences because of my travel due to my real estate career. Some favorite experiences include expedited entrance to the Skydeck at the Willis Tower in Chicago because I was meeting with the developer there; a spring home game at Nationals Stadium in Washington, DC; and a behind the scenes tour of the Dallas Cowboys stadium where I was able to stand on the field. I have had previews of various retail developments before they were open to the public, but they later go on to become a vibrant and indelible part of a community. I have eaten at restaurants before they experienced national success. Also, there are sometimes opportunities to see family and friends when visiting certain markets, which is always a bonus when it happens.

But business travel is also grueling. You always have a suitcase partially packed and ready to go. You may deal with changing time zones, which can be exhausting. You may get delayed by weather, by equipment malfunctions, by labor issues at airports or other more life changing events (such as when all the airports closed after the attacks of 9/11 or when cities began closing down in 2020 due to the global pandemic). You may be trying to complete important projects while traveling and you may have issues with internet connectivity which affects your ability to complete your work. The travel may also impact your ability to attend certain meetings or participate in conference calls. If you have children, an unexpected travel delay can mean missing out on certain aspects of their lives on a regular basis when you are not expecting it.

In brief, I always say the travel required in a corporate real estate position is a mixed blessing. Exhilarating and interesting at times. Difficult and draining at other times.

What are the greatest challenges you have faced in the industry?

There are many deal specific challenges that are faced daily. But my greatest challenge over time has been realizing that being in a corporate or franchise real estate position is actually a very solitary job.

It is a job where you have much collaboration with others, both internal and external to your company. However, there is frequently someone who is not satisfied with the results you deliver. A landlord will often want to find a way for you to pay them more rent; your company may want you to find a way to pay less rent. A company may want you to open more stores, but not be realistic about the time frames or budgets needed to accomplish this plan. At times a company may want the site that your competitor secured, even if they had the opportunity and passed on it for some reason in the past. Sometimes a franchisee expects you to have the magic answer to solve their lease or building issue. It is often easy for others to criticize the way a deal was structured or the way the negotiations proceeded, without ever being in the trenches during the negotiation process.

It makes those rare moments when you get a compliment from someone on how much you helped them or what a good site was obtained very sweet indeed! It also forces you to realize how strong you are as an individual; you get up every day and continue to push forward despite the pushback because when you do get a win, it is very satisfying.

What is the best negotiation tip you have learned?

My go to tip for negotiating is that if you do not ask, you will not know if it was attainable. Another way of thinking about this is that it is not a bad thing to politely offend the other side with your requests. The worst thing that they can say is "no." Since you know that is a possibility, if you obtain agreement to additional terms that you really pushed hard to obtain, even if you compromise and achieve slightly less than you originally asked, you have definitely come out in a better position than if you had not asked at all.

A second tip is that in a corporate real estate position, you always have the power to say no as well. You should walk away from the deal if you think you are not obtaining an acceptable outcome. Always remember that and you will always feel empowered.

What time management tools or skills do you use?

Effective time management is a huge goal and challenge of mine; at Propelled Brands, I am supporting multiple franchisees in multiple countries and various time zones. More than 700 franchisees have my name and know that they can reach out to me if they have a lease or development issues. I also have several direct reports and outsource vendors with whom I must interact frequently in order to keep projects on track. It feels as if there is never enough time in a day to react as thoroughly as I would like to all these individuals.

To stay organized, I rely heavily upon technology. Email, video calls, and messaging programs are all vital to managing my time and my ability to respond to people on a timely basis. For specific projects, I use a combination of old fashioned "To Do" lists (sometimes hand-written, sometimes typed) along with newer technology options such as the "Keep Lists" in Google, the snooze feature in email, and various project trackers. My company also uses template emails for recurring interactions that have similar follow up messaging. When needed, I make a calendar appointment with myself to accomplish activities which need a high degree of focus.

I like technology-based options as technology allows items to recirculate to the forefront of my attention based upon parameters that I have provided. However, I also like the feeling of marking something physically off a "To Do" list; so, for me, it remains a hybrid approach.

What advice would you give to the next generation of female leaders?

That being a great leader does not mean you need to think of yourself as a female, but it also does not mean that you need to forget that you are a female. Female leaders have some traits that male leaders may not have. Women are typically great listeners. Women are empathetic. Women have more often put in more time doing the detailed work over a longer period in order to advance, so they have a better grasp of the realities of the various jobs that make up the full spectrum of an organization.

Since many women still shoulder the majority of the responsibilities at home as well as full-time jobs, they are excellent multi-taskers and great at time management. In short, embrace the skills that are often found in female leaders, but do not focus on being a female. Focus your energies on being a great leader.

What organizations or groups do you recommend becoming part of your network?

There are many great organizations for real estate professionals. ICSC is a key one that I have always belonged to for many years. It has always offered great informational programming as well as networking opportunities. I think their virtual offerings are also a bonus, as they can sometimes be reviewed on your own time. However, there are other great organizations as well: NACORE, CREW, CoreNet, to name a few.

Local networking groups are also important. I am a member of Deals in Heels in Dallas which is a local group of female executives in the real estate industry (also, how I became part of this book project). This group of women gets together monthly for lunch and a meeting. The meetings usually feature a speaker that provides information on a specific retailer or a retail project or perhaps a larger city development objective. It is a great way to stay connected socially, but also to have an education component that improves your knowledge of the local market. I am also part of several less formal networking groups, which get together to exchange ideas and information from time to time.

As an individual who works in the franchise industry, there are other organizations such as the IFA (International Franchise Association) which are beneficial in providing both education and networking opportunities at annual conventions as well as at local events throughout the year.

Looking back, what is one thing you wish you knew at the beginning of your career?

A career in real estate will have a lasting impact on communities and on peoples' lives. Real Estate development literally changes the way communities evolve and the way people live their lives on a daily basis by bringing new retail concepts, restaurants, services and employers into the community. Most of the companies I have worked for have a franchising footprint. This is another way to have an interesting impact during the course of your career as helping franchisees build a business may in turn build generational wealth for their families. In brief, your impact as a Real Estate professional is immeasurable and long-lasting.

BIO - HOLLAND BURTON

Holland Burton is the Senior Director of Development Services for Propelled Brands. Propelled Brands is a multi-brand platform company which is the Franchisor of the FASTSIGNS, NerdsToGo, and My Salon Suite/My Salon Plaza brands. Holland oversees real estate, design, and construction activities for the FASTSIGNS and NerdsToGo concepts and has been with the company since January 2021.

Prior to joining Propelled brands, Holland worked for many iconic regional, national, and international restaurant and specialty food brands during her career, including: Corner Bakery Cafe and Il Fornaio (CBC Restaurant Corp.); La Madeleine Country French Café, Bruegger's Bagels, Timothy's Coffee, Michel's Baguette, and Mmmuffins (LeDuff America); Starbucks Coffee; Atlanta Bread Company; Cinnabon; The Coffee Beanery, Ltd.; Shoney's, Captain D'S and Lee's Famous Recipe Chicken (Shoney's, Inc.); Arby's; Wendy's; Taco Bell; and Popeyes Fried Chicken. Holland earned a Bachelor of Arts in French from the University of North Carolina at Chapel Hill and a Master's of International Management from the Thunderbird School of Global Management at ASU. Holland's background is diverse with site selection, lease negotiations, and development expertise in a variety of venues such as shopping centers, malls, street locations, free-standing buildings, and airports.

Holland currently lives in Allen, TX, and has 2 adult daughters, one in New York City and the other in Washington, D.C. She is an avid walker who enjoys reading, watching baking shows, listening to podcasts, traveling, and spending time with her family who are spread out across the country.

LYNN DOWDLE

Company: Dowdle Real Estate

Years in Commercial Real Estate: 31

How did you get started in commercial real estate and what age?

I relocated to Dallas from Oklahoma City in 1991. A single parent, with two young children, I transferred from a very lucrative position with a graphics company in OKC where I had been selling lettering machines to architects, engineers, etc. This was before computers were mainstream if you can imagine... I made top sales every year and was on every top producer trip that the parent company offered. Besides the success in my position, I loved the people I worked with, especially the owners of the business and their daughter who had become a very dear friend.

I transferred and began working with a different graphics company in DFW. Obviously, I came highly recommended by my past employers who hated to lose me. The problem I would run into was that the owners of this new company – a married couple - were not at all aligned with me and my principles. They were of different religious beliefs as me (I am a Christian) and put simply, they were not used to a powerful, successful woman so I came across as intimidating to the wife. I was sure I wasn't going to steal her husband, but she was not and I was sure to take heed quickly. I knew this was not I left in less than a year.

As I mentioned, I was a single parent with a then 9-year-old son and a 7-year-old daughter. What was I to do? I had no savings and no idea how this would unfold. But as I mentioned before, I was a woman of faith and so I began...I had a friend who was and still is a broker. Paula knew that after I left my work, I had to make a good living in order to provide for my children. She told me I should be in commercial real estate. I told her I knew nothing about it.

Back then, we lived near a beautiful park and every day after I took the kids to school, I would listen to inspiring podcasts while walking the woods. It felt good and quiet time had been hard to find so I cherished these times. Paula kept on encouraging me, I told her about my prayerful walks and one day she called to talk. She asked me what I had been doing and of course I said "walking in the woods" which may have sounded a bit strange. She told me that she wanted to introduce me to a man and to meet at a local restaurant. I had no idea what it was about, but I accepted, not knowing since I was trying to be open minded about my future. I met with this man named Dave. It was a short lunch with a lot of questions about my family, my wishes for the future, etc. I answered all of them as honestly as I could, I gave Dave my contact information and went about my business – back to walking and believing.

One day, I called a preacher friend of mine to tell him I was scared and that I was not at all sure about what my next move should be. Here is what he said – "Pray for the man to come into your path to bring you the job. And more than that – Pray for exactly what you need and want" I said okay. He said write it down – make a list of what you want. So, I did. I began to pray for the man to come into my path to bring me the job. And I made a list of what I wanted and more precisely what I needed to raise my kids the way I wanted to. It went like this 1) $40,000 per year salary (which was unheard of) but I was staying true to my needs. 2) I would learn new skills in order that I might have a long-term career and 3) That I would find joy in this work and my hands and feet would be busy. I prayed over this list until the call came.

One morning shortly after I had taken the kids to school, the phone rang, and it was Dave. He asked me what I was doing, and I told him I was about to go walk in the woods (really?). He said I am coming over. I remember feeling a strange sort of excitement and strangely asking him if he wanted orange juice or coffee. He said orange juice. The time after the call was slow motion at it is best. I had no idea what to expect but right when I started feeling nervous, the doorbell rang. I went to open the door and Dave walked deliberately through the door without a word. He went to the breakfast table where his orange juice was sitting and sat down, pulled out a yellow legal pad and started writing. I sat down across from him and felt confused at best. He finally stopped writing, folded the yellow paper in two and slid it over to me. He said,

"This is for you." I opened it up and the very first thing I saw was 1) $40,000.00 salary. 2) I was to learn the business to lease his shopping centers and 3) I would need to get my real estate license while working and learning the business. There it was! All the things I had specifically written down and prayed about delivered by a man named Dave who came into my path to bring me the job!

It was hard to wrap my head around, but it was the beginning of a long-term career that I would love and prosper from. Amen!

Do you have an industry specialty or niche?

I specialize in land sales. A good amount of my work is hotel site selection.

What advice do you have for someone entering the commercial real estate industry?

I always pull young people aside and tell them "If you will stay focused and work really hard, you will make life-time friends and you will have the time of your life." And keep in mind, "Overnight success happens in about 20 years." You can do great things – be patient.

Did/do you have a mentor and how did you find him or her?

I have had mentors in my career and those mentors know who they are. They come naturally for the most part, but I also asked several people who I respected if they would mentor me over the years. Every single time, the mentor accepted the role of my request unconditionally. I learned that most people are more than willing to help. I remind myself that regularly when I need someone's assistance – whether on a board, a committee or working a deal. People are kind and willing to help each of us succeed. I also give everyone an opportunity to mentor me daily. I look for qualities that I admire and aspire to in others and adopt those qualities as my own. You can do this too. It will give you an active role in becoming the woman you want to be.

What is the best advice you have received?

The best advice I have ever received, and I firmly believe it – "Nobody else knows what they are doing either." Read that again. Takes the heat off - right?

What are three skills you need to be in the industry?

You need to be a good listener. Many women are better listeners than their male counterparts. I have seen it repeatedly – in meetings, on the phone, negotiation, etc. We have the advantage on this one. Secondly, you need to have GRIT. The work is often hard, defeating, can feel like a lot of rejection and is very competitive. You have to stay in the game and figure out who you are in the game. You can't have a defeatist attitude, or the sharks will eat you for lunch. And third, be creative. That is the fun part. Create deals that aren't evident, that aren't easy and that maybe no one else would create. For me this is fun – watching a hotel come out of the ground while I have a huge smile on my face due to the fact that no one else would have gotten it done the way I did. Find joy in this. The joy keeps us going and it is the energy you will take to the next deal. Finding the joy is such an opportunity for many reasons – in work and life, that is.

What failure stands out for you and what did you learn?

I do not remember – whatever it was, I let it go. I learned and moved on. I would encourage you to do the same. Nobody needs a constant critic – especially if it is yourself! You take you wherever you go. That does not sound like a good way to spend your time. Let it go.

What are the steps you have taken to succeed in commercial real estate?

A lot of hard work, walking to my car after work in the dark, working on weekends, making cold calls, feeling like a kindergartener, experiencing joy driving down the tollway when I realized I was really "doing this," knocking on doors and attending networking to land new clients…All of these were deliberate yet baby steps, indeed. It is all a process. Trust the timing of your life and know that things will unfold as they are meant to. Bring 100% of you and your efforts and all the good stuff will come. Do not quit. If you quit, you will never have the same chances again. You have got to lean in, trust and know that great things are zooming your way!

What question are you asked the most?

Every question is different because it comes from an individual that is unique. This is where listening comes in. Listen until you know what the person who is asking really needs. This is where the good stuff happens.

What are the greatest challenges you have faced in the industry?

In the early days, it was a challenge to be in the good ol' boy club. Well actually – that is not the proper way to say that. The challenge was NOT being in the good ol' boy club at all. I don't feel this any longer because I feel as though the work that I've put in along with my leadership skills have spoken for themselves. I don't believe I'm looked upon as an underdog any longer.

Quite the contrary. I guess you could say I am no longer a girl trying to find her way in a man's world. I am now a woman who commands respect among the best of the best. I feel my strength, so others do too. I feel my competence and others yield to it too. I feel my uniqueness and others allow me to have the space that was meant for me. And may I say - It was well worth the journey.

What is the best negotiation tip you have learned?

It is a universal truth that a deal will never make until both parties are happy with the transaction. Then it is a WIN.

What time management tools or skills do you use?

Well at this point in my life, I take care of myself first. I know for sure that if I am not "filled up" I will have nothing to give my family, friends or clients. I set a "meeting" time to work out daily, I eat well, I get plenty of sleep and manage my emotions in a positive way – often through meditation or talking out my thoughts and feelings with a loved one. "Take care of yourself so you can take care of others" has been a mantra of mine for a very long time. You can hang your hat on it.

What advice would you give to the next generation of female leaders?

Please – for the love of God – do not try to be a guy! Dress like you want to dress as long as your attire is not too revealing. Express yourself in a real and authentic way which will probably not be a conversation similar to that of a dude. Talk about what matters to you, negotiate a deal in a way which you are proud of, and let others think what they will. Eventually you will stand apart from the guys. This is a beautiful thing. Authenticity wins every time. Be real and go for the gold.

What organizations or groups do you recommend becoming part of your network?

I have been involved for years with NTCAR and TREC. I am a big believer in networking, getting to know others in the industry and serving. Serving and giving to others will sustain you in your darkest hours. Find an organization you love and go all in.

Looking back, what is one thing you wish you knew at the beginning of your career?

Love yourself and be patient with yourself. Do your best every day and if you mess up forgive yourself and believe what I always remind myself and my now adult children "The sun will come out tomorrow." Be you. You can create the career you want and live this lovely life with great appreciation and gratitude while striving to give back. It does not get any better than that. And if there's anything I can do to help, come find me and ask me. I will be here for you. And, by the way, if you have read this to the end, I am very proud of you. You are on a roll – Enjoy the ride!

BIO - LYNN DOWDLE

PROFESSIONAL EXPERIENCE

Lynn is a recognized top producing real estate broker in the Dallas/Fort Worth Metroplex with extensive experience in hospitality site selection and land sales, restaurant, ground lease, build-to-suit and development opportunities. Prior to forming Dowdle Real Estate, she held Senior Vice President positions with SRS Real Estate Partners (formerly Staubach), The John Bowles Company, Trammell Crow Company and the Tara Group. Lynn's unique ability to foster long-lasting relationships, comprehensive background and astute business acumen has allowed her to become one of the most significant brokers in the Lone Star state. Lynn is a past long term member of the North Texas Commercial Association of Realtors and is Past President. Lynn sits on the Executive Board of Directors for TREC, is Past Chair of the TREC Leadership Committee, and is the 2022 Chair of Fight Night. She is a member of the NTCAR Hall of Fame Committee and Co-chaired the Hall of Fame Event in 2020. She is also an active member of the International Council of Shopping Centers.

PERSONAL INTERESTS

Lynn sits on the Circle of Friends Board with New Friends New Life, an organization which restores and empowers formerly trafficked girls and sexually exploited women and their children. Lynn is a past member of the Board of Directors of Our Friends Place, a safe - haven for neglected, abused or abandoned girls ages 10-17. She has been involved with the Teen Outreach Program and participates regularly in counseling misguided teens. Aligned with World Vision, Lynn is a founder of the organization "If You Knew", raising money for clean water in Africa (www.ifyouknew.org). Lynn has a daughter, Kelly, who is a model, actress, entrepreneur and singer/song writer in NYC. Her son, Joe, serves as Senior Vice President of the Land Division/Capital Markets in JLL's Austin office. He and his wife Jaclyn have 4-year old Griffin and 1- year old Goldie. Lynn's family is everything to her.

JENNIFER FRANK

Company: Segovia Partners

Years in Commercial Real Estate: 32

How did you get started in commercial real estate and what age?

My career in commercial real estate began as an intern focusing on office leasing for a newly formed Fort Worth firm called Huff, Brous, McDowell and Montesi when I was 20 years old. I was in college; leasing apartments and I met a mortgage broker who piqued my interest in the industry. Through a series of conversations and many introductions to leaders in the Dallas commercial real estate world, I landed an internship position in Fort Worth. Upon graduation in the early 1990s, the entire industry was in crisis which led me down a narrow path of opportunities in the business and brought me into the shopping center side of the industry to manage a package of RTC (Resolution Trust Corp) properties purchased by GE Capital.

Do you have an industry specialty or niche?

My niche in the industry is retail tenant representation and a deep knowledge of middle markets throughout Texas and the south as well as the major Texas markets.

What advice do you have for someone entering the commercial real estate industry?

My advice to people launching their careers in commercial real estate is to seek a mentor, create a "committee" of career and personal advisors, be part of a team or have a partner; be willing to work the hardest and accept the least credit, listen in on as many deal making conversations as you can, develop your own unique deal making personality, listen more than you talk and ask lots of questions. And try not to get discouraged when you hear "no" or deals fall apart – treat your experiences as learning opportunities; make adjustments as necessary and you will grow.

Did/do you have a mentor and how did you find him or her?

I had several mentors in the business and continue to seek mentors after 30 years in the industry. There is always someone who you can learn from. My best mentors have been clients.

What is the best advice you received?

The best advice I ever received was to learn to see my value as a broker and negotiate for myself. It has been said "If you can't negotiate for yourself, who can you negotiate for?" As a young broker, I was pushing hard to be a top producer and negotiate for perks - reimbursements, etc. My mentor suggested that I negotiate something much larger that depended on my earning capabilities. I gave up many reimbursable expenses in lieu of a larger commission percentage, betting on my abilities and it paid off. It taught me to believe in myself and gave me the confidence that led me to leave the safety of a larger firm and eventually start my own company.

What are three skills you need to be in the industry?

Three skills needed in the industry are networking, negotiation and resilience.

> ➤ **Networking** is especially important to developing long term relationships in an industry that is relationship based and long term.

> ➤ **Negotiation** skills are essential to a career in this industry. A great negotiator knows their audience and carefully navigates to a successful closing with both parties feeling like they have won.

> ➤ **Resilience** is key as you can run into many closed doors before one opens. Keep pushing!!

What failure stands out for you and what did you learn?

In 2010 during the recession, I was concerned about the future of real estate, and I felt that I needed to diversify. I franchised a restaurant chain and opened three sandwich stores. It was a huge failure, and I lost a lot of time, money and damaged some relationships in the process. It was the one of the most difficult times in my life. But I got through it with a lot of humility, faith and with help from a few incredible people. I learned that fear is a terrible motivator for me; it causes poor, irrational decisions. I now chose to deal with my fears head on and live in freedom from them to the best of my ability.

What are the steps you have taken to succeed in commercial real estate?

> Prioritize people over deals, building lasting relationships.

> Hard work. The commitment to go above and beyond.

> Staying surrounded by great people.

> Willingness to walk away from a client, deal or situation that is not a good fit.

> Create an inner circle of industry friends.

What question are you asked the most?

What prompted you to start your own brokerage company and how did you do it. And the answer is that "committee" I mentioned previously. Having an inner circle of friends both inside and outside of the industry helped me to navigate the process with confidence.

What are the greatest challenges you have faced in the industry?

Being a female in the industry in the late 1980's and into the 1990's when there were very few women in the industry was challenging. Breaking into the industry as a female required that I was not only a good "people person" but also had knowledge. I spent a lot of time learning my markets not only present conditions but what they would look like in the future and always studied up on the retail operation itself to better communicate with the decision-making team.

What is the best negotiation tip you have learned?

The best tip on negotiating is to be quiet and listen. The first one that speaks is usually the one who wants the deal the most and gives power to the silent.

What time management tools or skills do you use?

My best days begin with prayer and meditation along with some form of exercise. If I do these things, it gives me a sense of order for the day and allows me to manage my day. It is very important to prioritize your sense of wellbeing over the chaos of the day.

What advice would you give to the next generation of female leaders?

The best advice to future leaders is to have clear vision of what you want to accomplish, think strategically, work collaboratively and always treat people the way you want to be treated.

What organizations or groups do you recommend becoming part of your network?

ICSC has multiple communities and serving positions and is the gold standard for Shopping Center organizations, however, I think that a more local community of peers is key. Join or create a group of female CRE peers that can fuel your growth by sharing information, best practices, networking and help you to be in a strong community that supports you. Whatever you decide to become involved in be sure that you are aligned with the participants in values and vision and that you are able to commit time to this community and not just checking a box.

Looking back, what is one thing you wish you knew at the beginning of your career?

Looking back at my career, I wish I had been more purposeful to make investments in real estate from the start. It is easy as a broker to get swept in the current of the instant gratification of the commission-based business with checks coming in and expenses going out. It took me a few years to adopt the idea of using my own money to make money in the future.

BIO - JENNIFER FRANK

Jennifer Frank, Founding Partner of Segovia Partners, has 30 years' experience with national retail tenant representation and shopping center leasing. Tenant representation is her specialty throughout Texas, Arkansas, Louisiana and Oklahoma, where her talents range from small market placements to major market entries for big box retailers. In addition to her expertise on the tenant side, Ms. Frank has a successful track record for pre-leasing out of the ground developments as well as redevelopment projects.

Jennifer is consistently a top performer within the Dallas/Fort Worth market, being recognized by "Heavy Hitters" and D CEO. She is responsible for IKEA's market rollouts in the Dallas/Fort Worth, Austin and San Antonio. Additionally, Jennifer launched Staples market entry into Texas with over 30 stores and Conn's Appliances market entry into Dallas/Fort Worth and Oklahoma City with over 25 stores. Over the past two decades, Jennifer has led an aggressive expansion program for ULTA Beauty in Texas, Louisiana, Arkansas, and Mississippi, completing over 130 new store locations including the chain's top performing store. Jennifer's current clientele consists of Barnes & Noble, Skechers, EOS Fitness, Coffee Bean & Tea Leaf, Paper Source, IKEA, and ULTA Beauty. Her expertise in major rollouts, along with initial secondary market strategies is one of the many ways Jennifer offers value to her many clients. Today Jennifer remains focused on the Texas market and has partnered with Site Source Retail Brokers Network to serve her clients on a national platform.

Prior to forming Segovia Partners, Jennifer was allied with Princeton Partners, and for 17 years prior to that, she was with The Woodmont Companies where she was recognized multiple years as top producer and promoted to Executive Vice President. As EVP, she was responsible for new business development, national account representation and managing a team of over 15 brokers.

Pamela J. Goodwin

Company: Goodwin Commercial

Years in Commercial Real Estate: 36

How did you get started in commercial real estate and what age?

I have a degree in Interior Design from the University of Nebraska – Lincoln and my dream job was to be a hotel designer. At the age of 21, I was offered an interior design position with the JW Marriott in Bethesda, MD for $21,000 a year but I decided to turn the position down and stayed in my hometown of Omaha, NE working for an office developer as an in-house interior designer. I was a designer for only one year before accepting a project management position within the company and started working on a new shopping concept called "Power Centers" in 1988 that were being constructed in Arizona.

Part of my career I was working on large shopping center development projects and the other half I was working on the tenant side working for Brinker International which owned several restaurant concepts based in Dallas, TX. After developing more than 50 new Chili restaurants from the ground up for Brinker, in 2006 at the age of 42 I made the best decision ever to start my own commercial real estate firm *Goodwin Commercial* specializing in brokerage, consulting and development.

Do you have an industry specialty or niche?

As they say, "the riches are in the niches" and I found my niche developing, investing and selling single-tenant net lease pad sites EX: Walgreens, McDonalds, Chase, 7-Eleven tenants.

What advice do you have for someone entering the commercial real estate industry?

The best advice I have for someone entering the CRE industry is to find the best company and the top leaders in the industry and work for them when starting out in the business. I thought I wanted to open a restaurant so I researched best restaurant companies in the world and at the time it was Brinker International. I was paid to learn about the restaurant business and found out quickly I did not want to own the restaurant, I wanted to own the real estate.

When doing brokerage deals, most people assume you have to start off doing small tenant deals but I tell people you can start with large deals because it is the same amount of work.

Attend networking events and always arrive early for the event to meet the speakers and sit in the front. Do not just collect business cards, follow up with the people you meet and start building relationships. Write the date you met them on their business card along with where you met them and immediately add to your contact database. People do business with people they know, like and trust.

Did/do you have a mentor and how did you find him or her?

I had four main mentors during my career and they are:

➢ **Ted Zych (father)** – learned how to be an entrepreneur by making sure the customer/client was happy and to go above and beyond.

➢ **Sharon Zych (mother)** – You can do anything you want! My mom has been my biggest cheerleader and always took the time to listen to my crazy business ideas.

➢ **Jim Christon** – I met Jim while I was working at Brinker International and he was a preferred developer for Chili's. I approached him because he had more than 50 years of developing commercial properties and had an excellent reputation in the industry. I met with Jim and discussed my business plan to partner up on development deals together. He believed in me and helped start my own CRE business. We were business partners for four years developing properties with national tenants. He taught me how important it is to always write letters to people or send them an article they have appeared in. They will always remember you for doing something special by just writing a handwritten letter. It will go a long way!

➤ **Dan Lem** – I met Dan because we were looking for a broker to sell our Walgreens investment property and Dan was known throughout the industry to specialize in selling Walgreens throughout the country. That was his niche and made multi-millions in commission fees. He taught me about "selling the sizzle and not the steak" on a property. When I list my properties instead of having boring highlights I write about what stands out about the property. Dan recommended I have a salt-timer, like you find in a board game, when making prospective client calls and when the time was up, it was time to move onto the next phone call. Dan had me change an email from asking "What do *think* about making an offer?" to "How do you *feel* about making an offer?" You want the person to feel the emotion vs thinking about the offer.

I highly recommend having a coach or mentor throughout your career who is at least 10x's the level of your current level. Do your homework before you work with them and really make sure you know their professional history and where you want to be in the next level of your career. A person with integrity is key to me.

Remember if you pay for a coach or a mentor, you pay attention and it is well worth the learning experience. Anytime you find a coach or mentor and they agree to help you make sure you occasionally ask them if you can help them with professionally in any way. For example, you may be really good at social media and your coach or mentor may need help in that area so volunteer your time. Always offer something in return for their time.

What is the best advice you have received?

The best advice I have received in the CRE industry is to become the expert in one area and be the go-to person. You want to be a specialist and not a generalist. Like a general practitioner doctor vs a cardiologist. The pay can be significantly different.

Stay in your pond. Which means stay in one main area of your city. It takes too much time to move the boat and try to find a new place to fish every time. If you stay in the same pond, you will know where the fish are. I see too many real estate agents/brokers have a listing in one city and the next one could be 30 miles away. Find a market and know everything about that area and every property in that city.

What are three skills you need to be in the industry?

- ➤ **Persistence** – CRE is a very competitive industry and you need to stand out in the real estate market. It is the Rule of "7" which your prospect needs to "hear" from you at least 7 times before they will take action. You have to be creative to obtain their attention. I will send an email, do a video text, mail a card, DM a message on social media, tag them on LinkedIn are a few examples. Some of my clients and friends call me, "Persistent Pam."

- ➤ **Patience** – know that some deals can take only a few months and others can take years to complete. This is why you have to have a lot of deals in your pipeline.

- ➤ **Positive** – this is a business with a lot of ups and downs and you have to keep a positive attitude. One day you are on cloud nine because you closed on a deal and the next you lost a big deal. If you have to stay at a steady pace so you do not get burned out in this business.

What failure stands out for you and what did you learn?

One failure I experienced during my CRE career was not acquiring a piece of property because I listened to other people telling me the property was too expensive to acquire and a tenant would never pay that amount in a ground lease. It costs me millions of dollars by listening and not doing the development deal. I showed them and the next similar deal that came along and people told me it was too expensive, I actually purchased it with a business partner and we sold the property at an extremely high price. Trust your gut in this business!

What are the steps you have taken to succeed in commercial real estate?

➢ Pick up your phone and answer it – CRE agents have a reputation of not returning calls.

➢ Always work for the best companies – learn from the best.

➢ Fortune is in the follow up – set up a lunch, write a letter and build relationships with people. This is a relationship business.

➢ Learn from top people and always be a lifetime learner – continue to read books, attend networking events, watch YouTube videos, listen to podcasts, or start your own podcast or tv show. Readers are leaders.

➢ You have to pay to pay attention – when you pay a coach or trainer you learn more if you pay.

➢ If you are not waking up on Mondays loving what you do you are not in the right job or position and need to make a change

➢ Create a LLC so you can write off deductions when you travel for business or buy property. Have the best CPA for your personal and business transactions.

➢ Collaboration is key - you cannot build and grow without teaming up with the right people. Do not try to do it all alone because you can only do so much and will get burned out quickly.

What question are you asked the most?

I get asked the most, "How do you get started in commercial real estate." After developing more than 50 plus pad sites for Brinker International for new ground up Chili's and On the Border restaurants I found that landlords were making more than $800,000 on selling a 10-year ground lease with Chili's. Just like McDonald's is a billion-dollar real estate company and only flipping burgers to pay the rent.

A lot of people feel they need to start in residential and later transition to commercial. I do not advise that at all. Pick one that you like and stick with it. Do not try to do both. You would not want me selling your home.

What are the greatest challenges you have faced in the industry?

Some of the biggest challenges I have faced have been just the ups and downs of the economy over more than 30 years in the industry. Being a female in a male dominated industry you must prove yourself and gain credibility. Even today I can go to a meeting and still be the only woman at the table or in the room but I can guarantee you I will be more prepared than most people.

There are a lot of deals that end up never happening and you have to realize that going into this business. You have to be able to pick yourself up and move on quickly.

What is the best negotiation tip you have learned?

The best negotiation tip I have learned is that everything is negotiable and to always do your homework and be prepared. In this business "time kills deals" so do not negotiate for too long or you will lose the deal.

What time management tools or skills do you use?

I have learned to set up a routine each day and try to stay on track every day. I wake up around 6:00am and make my coffee and listen to morning prayer on YouTube videos, I write in my journal, write my "I Am" affirmations, what I am grateful, blessed and thankful for each day. If I do not do this every morning my day is thrown off. It is a priority. I time block and know I do my best work in the morning for follow up emails and calls.

Regarding time management, if someone requests to meet with me, I will only meet on Friday mornings or late afternoons and I will not schedule anything else for that day. Make sure you are consistent with your time management skills and focus on your top three main goals. If someone asks you to do something and it does not involve one of those goals, you should politely tell that person you are not available.

What advice would you give to the next generation of female leaders?

➢ Make sure you are asking if you can invest early on any real estate investments

➢ Go to your city website and find out how you can be involved in your community

➢ Start a podcast or tv show to share your knowledge and expertise

➢ Post on social media platforms informative videos every day

➢ Meet or call executive level people what career advice they can share

➢ Start your own networking group and meet monthly or quarterly for breakfast or lunch

What organizations or groups do you recommend becoming part of your network?

There are a lot of excellent groups to join and start networking to meet people in the industry. Do not just be a member but get involved and be on a committee in the group. I recommend:

➢ ICSC

➢ Deals in Heels (Dallas group only)

➢ Retail Live

➢ NTCAR

➢ Chamber of Commerce in your city

Check out your city website and get involved in your community by volunteering. After attending Planning & Zoning and City Councils meetings, I wanted to give back to my community, I submitted my application for the Zoning Board of Adjustments. I was selected by the mayor and now hold the position of Chair.

Looking back, what is one thing you wish you knew at the beginning of your career?

I would have started investing a lot earlier in my career and to think a lot BIGGER from the beginning. We are taught we must slowly work our way up to the top that can take years to accomplish. I tell people that it is the same process to sell a $5 million dollar property as it is to sell a $50,000 property.

Have systems and processes in place. Find and use the best database to keep track of contacts and follow up systems.

Have fun every day!

BIO - Pamela J. Goodwin

Pam Goodwin's interest in entrepreneurship started when she was four years old. Her first venture was a lemonade stand, and then worked in the family's poultry business, to tenant coordination/project management with several large shopping center owners, to developing more than 50 pad sites with Brinker Int. (Chili's and On the Border).

Pam is the CEO of Goodwin Commercial based in Plano, TX, an award-winning commercial real estate and consulting firm. With more than three decades of experience in development, buyer/tenant representation, project management, leasing, property development, 1031 exchanges, due diligence, and entitlements.

She graduated from the University of Nebraska-Lincoln (yes, big Cornhusker football fan). She is a published author of two books *One Cent Lemonade to Million Dollar Deals-25 Jobs & 25 Lessons I Wish I Learned Sooner! and an Amazon Best Seller for "Winning Ways in Commercial Real Estate."* Pamela created a four-part audio series "How to Win in Commercial Real Estate – Zero to $1,000,000 with One Deal."

She is a breast cancer survivor and is on a mission to spread the word all women should get an annual 3D mammogram instead of the standard 2D mammogram. Pam is the co-founder of "Kiss Breast Cancer Goodbye" an annual event in Nashville, TN since 2021 and to date has raised more than $227,000 for Susan G Komen to end breast cancer.

In her spare time, she enjoys spending time with her husband Eric and two sons Grant and Garrett, traveling, visiting family in Croatia and working out.

Contact Info:

Website: www.pamgoodwin.com

email: pam@pamgoodwin.com

SHARON HERRIN

Company: Herrin Commercial Real Estate

Years in Commercial Real Estate: 44 years

How did you get started in commercial real estate and what age?

I started my real estate career in 1979 after starting in the stock brokerage business where I was studying to be a stockbroker. I was in my mid-20's and one of the men I worked with went into real estate and offered me a job as his administrative assistant. From there I grew to love the business, went on to work with a developer of multi-family, retail, office, and land development, where I honed my skills and absorbed all the knowledge I could. After 23 years there, I started my brokerage career and then my own business.

Do you have an industry specialty or niche?

My niche/specialty has been working on special use property and restaurant dispositions. That was after 17 years of working in the property management side of the business. I ran a management company for an owner/developer of 3,000 multi-family properties, retail, and office, and then gravitated to brokerage. That experience in management gave me a better perspective when negotiating deals for both owners and tenants.

What advice do you have for someone entering the commercial real estate industry?

Learn as much as you can from every professional in this business, always ask questions, and be like a sponge and soak up all the knowledge you can. Seek out, meet people smarter than you, and learn from them. Take courses, educate yourself in specialties that will help you in your career path, but also always be curious and gain knowledge about all aspects of the business. Knowing many industry professionals will lead to introductions and business.

Did/do you have a mentor and how did you find him or her?

Yes, and my mentor was also my sponsor. The developer with whom I worked encouraged me to learn everything I could about every deal we put together.

When his partner left him without a development partner, he came to me and told me that we were both going to pick up and learn what needed to be done to finish the development and he needed me to step up and help. I found he was learning, and I was learning with him! He involved me in meetings, negotiations, and spent time reviewing documents in all transactions to teach me what he knew.

I encourage anyone to find your mentor(s) and then find a sponsor(s) that will get you in front of decision makers. That leads to opportunities for the rest of your life. What I learned is that a sponsor can validate your capabilities and sing your praises if you have worked hard, and they have witnessed that you can do the job. In return those clients they introduce you to have confidence you can do that job and that leads to business.

What is the best advice you have received?

To live by the golden rule, **ALWAYS** treat everyone, as you would wish to be treated.

What are three skills you need to be in the industry?

> - Be a relationship builder and a connector, those relationships are forever and bring business to you and those connections you make both with and to others pay off.

> - Be a good listener, you cannot help others without listening to their needs.

> - Be a giver of your time and energy. You get what you give.

What failure stands out for you and what did you learn?

My failure was admitting I had made a major error in a lease negotiation and going to my owner to tell them I had made that error. Admitting the error was frightening, but gathering my courage to discuss my error was the best thing I ever did. I learned my owner had a deeper respect for my having laid out what I did without "discovering" the error and I learned it could be addressed professionally and still save the tenant relationship and get the deal done. Admitting your errors and taking responsibility were what I learned was the best road to always take. It gains you confidence and respect.

What are the steps you have taken to succeed in commercial real estate?

Aligned myself with those that are excellent in their fields of expertise, aligned myself with others wiser than me, and soaked up all the knowledge that I could by learning constantly. If you align with others more skilled, you learn and get better in your profession. Find those that you admire and are successful and learn from them.

What question are you asked the most?

What would I do differently now that I know today what I did not know then?

What are the greatest challenges you have faced in the industry?

Learning to adapt and change directions in the downturns in the market. There are and always will be downturns and reverses in the economy and our real estate industry. Lesson learned is to prepare for those downturns, do not rely on the market always being on the upswing, put money back when times are good to help when they are not so good.

What is the best negotiation tip you have learned?

Listen to what the other side is telling you they need and continue to listen to bring all parties together, you are never going to get everything you want, but neither is the other side, and you need to walk away feeling you have done the best for your client with them feeling the same way.

What time management tools or skills do you use?

Time management is always one of the hardest to control. In this business, a day can start with the best of intentions of addressing priorities and then those priorities change. I end the day making a list of those items I did not address and reassess their priority and start over the next day. You need to have a realistic understanding that flexibility is going to be what keeps things rolling.

What advice would you give to the next generation of female leaders?

Invest in yourself, seek out mentors and sponsors and in turn pay it forward.

What organizations or groups do you recommend becoming part of your network?

Commercial Real Estate Women (CREW), International Council of Shopping Centers (ICSC), North Texas Association of Commercial Realtors (NTCAR), Urban Land Institute (ULI), The Real Estate Council (TREC). Small groups yet important for networking are those that reflect your expertise, i.e. I belong to a networking group of highly skilled brokers that are in the retail world called Deals in Heels and Independent Broker Alliance, a group of individuals that are small to mid-size business owners.

I highly recommend becoming a member of professional groups. CREW, a global network of 12,000 members in all disciplines of commercial real estate is my group of choice and it has been instrumental in building my network, my leadership skills, forming my company, and providing professional expertise to my clients. The return on your investment in these organizations is only as good as how involved you become.

Looking back, what is one thing you wish you knew at the beginning of your career?

To invest in real estate. Wish I had started earlier!

BIO - SHARON HERRIN

Sharon Herrin, principal of Herrin Commercial Real Estate, has spent over 44 years in commercial real estate. Her expertise spans a career in numerous real estate disciplines among which are owner representation, tenant representation, project leasing, retail, office and multi-family development, management and investment brokerage. Sharon's understanding of this broad range of real estate specialties brings knowledge, experience and strong skills that are beneficial to servicing her clients.

Sharon currently is serving on the Board of Directors of NTCAR, has served as a Global CREW Network Board Director (2017-18), CREW Network Foundation Board Chair (2018-19), is a Past President of CREW Dallas (1999), and is a CREW Network Foundation Visionary. Sharon is a recipient of the CREW Dallas Outstanding Achievement Award (2001), CREW In the Community Award for Philanthropic Excellence (2015), the CREW Dallas 2021 Business Collaboration Award, and the CREW Network 2022 Impact Award for Member-to-Member Business and is a CREW Dallas Life Member.

Sharon has served on the Boards of numerous non-profits including LaunchAbility, The Dallas Women's Foundation, Plano Chapter of the Susan G. Komen Foundation and The Dallas Summer Musicals Guild.

Sharon is a native Texan and native Dallasite.

DANIELLE KAUFMAN

Company: DMKC, LLC d/b/a Kaufman Consultants

Years in Commercial Real Estate: 15 Years

How did you get started in commercial real estate and what age?

I was 21 years old when I started my career in commercial real estate. I was an Accounting Major at the University of Cincinnati, actively involved in the university's co-op program when I secured an internship at The Kroger Co. The internship program offered a rotational sequence where each intern could experience working in a different department relevant to their field of study. I began in the Tax Department and then transitioned to Accounting. The pre-determined rotation would have placed me in Capital Management/Finance, except that I received candid feedback from my supervisor challenging me to reconsider my career path.

It was the standard process to receive a review from your supervisor before leaving a department. He told me that whereas I was good at accounting, my supervisor was honest when he said to me that he did not think the position was a good fit for me and my extroverted personality. He explained that he thought I would get bored with the monotony of a cyclical career in accounting where the tasks required for period close, quarter close, and annual close would always remain the same. Completely confused, I asked, "What do you suggest I do?" He told me that the Real Estate Department used to have interns but had not participated in the program for several years. He thought I might enjoy working in a field that allowed me to get out of the office instead of being stuck in a cubicle.

Immediately following that meeting, I got on the elevator and introduced myself to the VP of Real Estate. I told him that I was an intern in accounting and interested in working in Real Estate. After several weeks had passed, the company offered me an opportunity to work in Portland, OR, where I learned critical market research and data analytic skills. I produced sales models for potential new stores, expansions, and remodels throughout the company marking the beginning of my commercial real estate journey.

Do you have an industry specialty or niche?

I specialize in ground-up retail development. I approach all projects with a strong focus on strategy, starting with the desired result and quickly determining what obstacles must be overcome. First, I develop and lead teams of highly qualified professionals to engineer the site from civil and architectural design. Next, we work together to secure property entitlements and permits for construction. In addition, I manage the entire construction process, from bidding to selecting a General Contractor and providing oversite through construction completion.

What advice do you have for someone entering the commercial real estate industry?

There are so many avenues:

➢ Brokerage

➢ Leasing

➢ Property Management

➢ Sales

➢ Development

➢ Investments

➢ The list goes on.

Find the role that challenges you and motivates you. That is where you will find happiness and success.

Did/do you have a mentor and how did you find him or her?

Of course! A mentor is someone you trust, whom you invite to get to know you, your challenges, and your goals. The relationship can develop into a lifelong friendship or only last until a specific purpose is achieved.

Valerie DeCaro – We met on the playground 30 years ago, and as deep as our friendship goes, we are complete opposites. Whether personal or professional, we are sure to complete a full list of pros and cons. I value her opinion and trust her to support me in my decisions. Even though it has been 15 years since we've lived in the same state, she's still the friend I call first for advice or to celebrate with.

Russell Cowart – Russell was one of the few counterparts who offered to help me if I had questions when I first started at Kroger. He explained processes and procedures and provided reasons when I questioned direction. We should have been each other's competition; however, we did not pursue the same opportunities. He knew I wanted to be the best. Russell encouraged me to apply for every job posting and celebrated my successes. His mentorship was a constant source of guidance throughout my corporate career, even though we never worked in the same office.

Jim Freeman – When we started working together, I had been with the company for five years, and Jim had nearly forty. Jim had an incredible ability to build relationships and rapport. He taught me the importance of getting to know someone and caring about them genuinely. His positive outlook on life made any lousy day better. I could talk to him about friendships, family, work, marriage, parenting, goals, failures, and achievements. No matter what soapbox I was standing on, he would listen and share the wisdom that placed any scenario in a positive light.

Nicholas Kaufman – If there is anyone who pushed me and continues to push me to succeed, it is my husband. We met at a leadership conference in Houston. Nick encourages me to set annual goals. We both set personal and professional goals as a couple. For example, in 2019, my goal was to find a new job, although I had no interest in another corporate role. Nick, a small business owner, encouraged me to create my own business. He continued to follow up until I finished the strategic plan. He helped me set up an LLC, design a logo, and other essential steps to launch Kaufman Consultants.

What is the best advice you have received?

As a direct communicator, I was advised to take a moment to understand my audience and self-edit before delivering a statement.

Only some people are receptive to direct communication, and the delivery can often be perceived as rude. Providing more detail than what you believe is necessary to will facilitate constructive two-way communication may be beneficial.

What are three skills you need to be in the industry?

> **Persistence** - The one thing you cannot control is making others respond. It can be very frustrating knowing that you cannot force someone to pick up the phone to call you back or type a reply to an email. Therefore, it is essential to follow up until your request has been fulfilled. For example, suppose it takes several messages to generate a response. In that case, every follow-up must be respectful and concise, which is much better received than the perception of being too pushy or demanding.

> **Likeability** - A social skill that is not just about being nice; it requires sincerity and honesty. Because Commercial Real Estate can only partially be learned from textbooks-observing and asking questions is crucial. Approaching everyone like they have something they can teach you is a great way to grow likability. When you ask a person to share their expertise, you will receive excellent advice and show genuine interest in that person's strengths.

> **Critical Thinking** - Every deal is different. A commercial real estate professional must be able to apply learnings from previous projects to future projects. The application of the learnings may change, but the thought process is the same. Not all land is created equal. Land may be flat, hilly, may have a stream running through it, or contaminated soils. Some variables could change the way a property gets developed. The goal is to analyze the obstacles that encumber the land and determine the most cost-effective way to design and build. All land can be created, but at what expense?

What failure stands out for you and what did you learn?

I experienced failure and learned a few life lessons in 2016, the year I ran a marathon. I attempted this goal previously and was unsuccessful. However, this was the year I was determined to finish.

As a result of my determination, I failed to sustain a work-life balance. My training schedule often resulted in a late start at the office and early departures. The reduced hours at work were manageable until my Assistant Manager unexpectedly went on medical leave. I had two new employees in the office that required much guidance, so I needed more support picking up the work left behind. Eight weeks into my training, I told my boss, "I am failing," overwhelmed with responsibility. I acknowledged that there was too much on my plate but failed to make any changes. My responsibility as a leader was to provide my employees with all the tools and coaching necessary to succeed. Five days a week, I spent hours at the ball fields supporting my son and his joy of playing baseball. My husband and I hardly saw each other as it was, so there was no time to spare. I could have given up on my goal, but I was unwilling to quit again.

Four weeks from Race Day, I was physically and mentally exhausted and failed to recognize that these symptoms can have significant health concerns. My Assistant Manager had returned to work, lifting the world's weight off my shoulders. Unfortunately, my mental state continued to decline. I was experiencing short-term memory loss and a sudden inability to focus. My eyes were open, but my mind was asleep in a daydream. I started napping during my lunch break but did not feel better or worse until two days before the marathon. I had vertigo so severe that I could not see or walk unassisted. In my case, the doctor's diagnosis was Chronic Fatigue, also referred to as Runners Fatigue. It could last for days, weeks, or even months; rest is the only cure. Although not recommended, I was told I could run if I could see straight the morning of the race.

I slept for 48 hours, missing work, a Christmas Party, and a friend's marriage proposal. Then, when I woke up on Race Day, although feeling sluggish, I walked without stumbling for the first time in two days. My husband drove me to the starting line and appeared every five miles along the course to cheer me on with friends. I snapped a picture at mile marker 20, the furthest distance I had run during my first attempt two years prior. Finally, after 4 hours and 43 mins, I crossed the finish line at 26.2 miles!

I celebrate this achievement not only for what it was but because only I can understand the strength it took to finish. I had pushed ALL of myself to its limits that year. However, having found those limits, I can more effectively manage my time, tolerance, and health with future endeavors. There are no actual failures, only life lessons.

What steps have you taken to succeed in commercial real estate?

I have stayed flexible and approached every opportunity with an open mind. I do not chase the dollar but analyze how each promotion would affect my career goals and lifestyle. I review the dynamics of each office before accepting a new role. It is crucial to understand if there is an opportunity for future advancement and set new expectations for the next promotion. Never be complacent. Complacency will only hold you back from realizing your full potential.

What question are you asked the most?

How did you get to Texas? While in college at the University of Cincinnati, I started my career with The Kroger Co. Then, I moved to Portland, OR for a summer, gaining work experience in the company's Corporate Research and GIS department. Next, I returned to Cincinnati to finish my degree. After graduation, I accepted the Real Estate Specialist position at Smith's Food & Drug, a Kroger subsidiary, and moved to Salt Lake City, UT. Later, I was promoted and relocated to Kroger's Mid-Atlantic division in Roanoke, VA. Finally, I earned another promotion that brought me to Dallas, TX. I had moved three times within three years, and as the saying goes, "I got here as quick as I could!"

What are the greatest challenges you have faced in the industry?

The volatility of the real estate market causes significant fluctuations in commercial development. Professionals must be prepared to stop on a dime and change direction. For example, retailers can go from opening 2-3 stores yearly to 10-15 or more, changing to an aggressive strategy overnight. With a sense of urgency, brokers and developers race to secure opportunities in strategic locations. When the market shifts and aggressive growth plans revert to normal, it causes a sudden halt in real estate transactions. Deals previously considered then must be renegotiated or terminated entirely. Understanding historical market trends can assist professionals in this industry in preparing for the ebbs and flows of the business. Be flexible. Be ready.

What is the best negotiation tip you have learned?

Good negotiation is a win-win, which requires both parties to make concessions. To be most effective, determine what is most important to you and the person you are negotiating with. Then, decide what you are willing to give up, and win what creates the most value for you. But, of course, creating value can be something other than money.

What time management tools or skills do you use?

One of the ways I manage my time is by combining calendars. My work, personal, husband's, and son's calendars are all separate but merged so I can view them together. In addition, I add tasks to my calendar, such as workout, reading for 30 minutes, calling a friend, and any appointments and social plans. It contributes to achieving a healthy work-life balance. As a result, I have better control over when work and personal events get scheduled, preventing over-booking, and planning for the necessary time needed to transition to each obligation.

What advice would you give to the next generation of female leaders?

Studies show that men dominate 75% of the conversation during conference meetings. I am frequently the only woman seated at the table in this male-dominated industry, making this statistic more apparent. The sooner you build your confidence to speak up, the sooner *you* will dominate and succeed in your career. Do your research before meetings and write down your thoughts or questions for discussion. If you have an idea and are still determining how somebody will receive it, share it with someone you trust. Seek feedback from a mentor, which will boost confidence when presenting. Finally, be intentional about saying anything at the beginning and end of every meeting, whether the discussion is business or casual. Your participation level may vary from meeting to meeting, but practice speaking up and making your presence known. This will grow your confidence and help you to be more assertive when the time calls for it.

What organizations or groups do you recommend becoming part of your network?

➢ Alumni Organizations

➤ Deals in Heels – Women in Commercial Real Estate

➤ Local Young Professional Groups

➤ Local Women in Business Organizations

➤ ICSC

Looking back, what is one thing you wish knew at the beginning of your career?

I wish I had known that learning from poor and great leaders is equally important. Unfortunately, there will be a time when you are led by management who exhibit destructive behaviors to the team's morale and productivity. However, this is not a reason to quit and move on, at least not immediately. Instead, use the unfortunate experience to learn first-hand what not to do. First, differentiate the characteristics between good leadership and bad leadership. Then, when you find yourself in a position to lead, remember the consequences that occurred because of bad leadership and demonstrate the qualities of an excellent leader to motivate others to achieve a strategic goal.

BIO - DANIELLE KAUFMAN

Danielle Kaufman has a bachelor's degree in accounting focusing on Real Estate and 15 years of commercial real estate experience in the grocery/retail industry. She founded Kaufman Consultants, a woman-owned real estate consulting company focused on bringing extensive retail background and development strategy to the vision of private developers and municipalities across Texas and Oklahoma. She is also a co-owner of a restaurant and winery, Wine Fusion Winery. Her entrepreneurial skills make her an expert in business management, networking, leadership, time management, and efficient execution. Danielle lives in Grapevine, Texas with her husband and stepson. She enjoys running, cooking, and experiencing new cultures around the world.

LESLIE J. MAYER

Company: Cushman & Wakefield

Years in Commercial Real Estate: 40

How did you get started in commercial real estate and what age?

I "unofficially" began my career as a child growing up in one of the most beautiful cities in the world, San Francisco, California. I was fascinated by all the landmark buildings and distinct districts such as the Golden Gate Bridge and Park, Coit Tower, Fisherman's Wharf, Union Square, Lombard Street, and Pacific Heights to name a few. By the use of those monikers, you could quickly distinguish the demographics of the people that frequented those places. I loved how different areas were defined by their signature landmarks. This is when I first learned the power of real estate and how "location, location, location" does matter. Remember how you always knew which neighborhoods had the best Halloween candy or holiday lights?

Officially, my career started when I was 21 as a senior in college working part-time for a commercial real estate developer. It gave me the opportunity to see how a project evolved from the ground up through design, financing, acquisition, construction, and sales/leasing. Once again, I was fascinated by the business and process of making and leaving behind a lasting physical imprint on the landscape that influenced how people lived, worked, and shopped.

Do you have an industry specialty or niche?

I have built my real estate practice around tenant representation primarily for retail and restaurant concepts. Most notably I have been the National Master Broker for two publicly traded footwear retailers as well as numerous regional restaurant groups.

What advice do you have for someone entering the commercial real estate industry?

Evaluate your short and long-term career objectives early on and ensure that there is passion and enthusiasm about the specialization in a particular field (e.g., leasing, sales, development, design, finance). I originally thought I wanted a career in advertising and to get a MBA. By doing various internships during college, I realized I did not really like the profession and ended up pursuing a career path in real estate instead because it resonated with me. I could have invested a lot of time doing something I disliked had I not gotten an inside look early on. Getting that exposure during college and summers will help confirm or redirect your professional focus so you can find something you truly enjoy doing and will excel at.

Did/do you have a mentor and how did you find him or her?

Women in a commercial real estate was still in its formative years when I started so I unofficially sought out various "teachers" based on who I emulated or wanted to learn from. I observed successful, reputable business processes and gleaned the best practices from a variety of professionals I admired regardless of whether they were men or women.

I was not "one of the guys," therefore I had to craft my own approach doing what was comfortable for me. I have since been a mentor for numerous young men and women and while there is still a different approach for women, gender is becoming less of a dividing line as we move forward with embracing diversity and inclusivity in our industry.

What is the best advice you have received?

My father always said to me, "Keep swinging kid!" which meant always give your best effort, understanding some days you hit it out of the park and other days you go back to the bench. No one scores 100% of the shots they take, but if you do the work to get in the game then you have the right to be there and contribute. I found that by being knowledgeable and anticipating variables that might occur, you can be nimble and quick in your response. That said, the best piece of advice I would give as a result is be prepared but "Don't guess," if you do not know the answer, say so but that you will get the information and revert back. It may be embarrassing, but it also prevents someone else from relaying or relying on incorrect information that can be passed along the management chain. Remember *You are your brand*.

What are three skills you need to be in the industry?

Today there is access to comprehensive empirical data and information through a variety of sources: Placer AI, targeted demographic studies, Co-Star/LoopNet and various other paid and unpaid subscription and data mining services. Artificial Intelligence will soon be part of decision making as well. Correspondingly, being able to comprehend and utilize these resources, will enable you to expand your anecdotal abilities and knowledge base and stay with or ahead of the trends.

But overall, always take action:

➢ **Read** as many periodicals related to your area of expertise or geography

➢ **Attend** or **Volunteer** at industry events and participate (e.g.: Crew, Chamber of Commerce, University sponsored Real Estate Groups/Clubs) in groups that further your business contacts and exposure

➢ **Listen** to relevant webinars and podcasts when you have free time.

➢ **Write** for or **Speak** at some of the above mentioned options

➢ **Be** a mentor within your company or college for a younger associate student.

➢ **Do** follow up and stay in touch with prospects and clients.

What failure stands out for you and what did you learn?

Early on, I was disappointed when I was not hired for a position with a specific real estate firm. My regret was based on my perception of the company as an industry leader. I had actually dodged a bullet, as they were shortly exposed for inappropriate business behavior. It made me appreciate the importance of doing **thorough due diligence** on people, places, and things before you give them credit or reverence.

What are the steps you have taken to succeed in commercial real estate?

I realized early on that I enjoyed commercial real estate. There seemed to be a natural fit with the retail side of the industry and the opportunity to be forward thinking and creative. It gave me exposure to neophyte companies and entrepreneurs and having the chance to help them grow into "bricks-and-mortar" sites was extremely rewarding.

I have been fortunate to have worked for my own company and with larger corporate firms representing retailers/restaurateurs and landlords. This has shown me the importance of building a cohesive team and growing a strong professional brand. Your reputation proceeds you so make it a good one!

What question are you asked the most?

"If you could do anything over again, what would you do differently??"

Answer: I would learn more about the intricacies of capital markets financing and analysis. The ability to fund something properly makes or breaks a deal.

What are the greatest challenges you have faced in the industry?

For me, it has been economic challenges. There have been several pivotal financial setbacks in the real estate industry in the last 20 plus years from: September 11, 2001, to the Wall Street mortgage market collapse and the "Great Recession of 2008", to Covid shutdowns in 2020-2022 and now the ever-higher interest rates of 2023 and Climate Change.

I have had to stay educated and forward thinking to ensure that my business was properly positioned to weather the uncertainties yet still be an asset to my clients by providing current market knowledge and assist them in making prudent decisions and formulate strategies.

While every past generation has had its own set of challenges, going forward, I believe that we will **all** be addressing issues in the form of utility shortages, and higher costs, scarcity of real estate options both residential and commercial combined with the upheaval in global supply chains, shifting politics and the increased presence of Artificial Intelligence ("AI"). Find ways to see/create the opportunities in these situations.

What is the best negotiation tip you have learned?

LISTEN Let the client really explain their objectives so that you can understand and deliver the results but ask questions as well to confirm that that they are adequately prepared to follow through to a successful conclusion. For example: "Do you have proper financing in place? Is your concept ready to launch? Do you have all your legal documents in place? Who/what is your competition and what have they done that you want to replicate or avoid? What is your timing.? Do you have a team assembled? By completing your due diligence on the client, you ensure that everyone's expectations are the same and can be met at the outset. Conversely, **LISTEN** to what the other side wants and needs to make sure that there is a fit. You do not want any surprises, and **both** sides should feel like winners.

What time management tools or skills do you use?

This is a great question, and it varies from task to task, especially in the new hybrid work environment post Covid. I work with an exceptional associate with whom I discuss our projects and objectives on a daily/weekly basis, and we prioritize, collaborate and set-up timetables for completion. We divide up the tasks based on who the best person is to complete the job.

If you do not have an associate or teammates, make your own list of priorities and obligations. Checking them off daily is an accomplishment within itself and it is harder to ignore tasks when they are written down. Using the alarms and calendar on your phone is a great way to remind yourself of upcoming meetings and dates too.

What advice would you give to the next generation of female leaders?

Today's young women have been the beneficiaries of seeing their own mothers work at various careers. Companies, too, are now accommodating women's needs so that you do not have to choose between having a family and/or a career.

I advise young women to make their professional and personal lives full and rewarding. Most of my female friends consider their work to be a big, but not exclusive part of who they are, separate and apart from their personal lives. If you take time off in your career, stay involved or educated in your field so if/when you return you are not starting from scratch. Technology continues to evolve so embrace it and learn how to use it to your advantage.

What organizations or groups do you recommend becoming part of your network?

There are numerous local/regional and national real estate and college groups, many of them oriented towards women, although I think it is best to join the ones that you will commit to participating in/with. Get your real estate license early on so you can be a more asset to a firm when you start.

I am a big proponent of volunteering or joining a Board of a local non-profit group that you are passionate about. You will not only meet like-minded people but often it is a great networking opportunity with other professionals who may need or refer your services.

Looking back, what is one thing you wish you knew at the beginning of your career?

Do not be afraid to *ask questions*. Participate in conversations. Sit in the front in classes and meetings. Befriend the administrative staff. Always dress for the job you want not necessarily in the latest fashion. (Always have comfortable close toed shoes at hand for site-walks).

Know who you are meeting with in advance and try to find a personal connection. I do not have children or play golf, but I do have dogs and a cat, and everyone loves to talk about their pets 😊

Establishing that personal rapport helps create a more genuine dialogue and relationship.

Most importantly "Never forget to ask for what you want for you or your client and always follow-up and close the deal!" Too many people lose opportunities because they were not clear in articulating what they wanted or needed.

BIO - LESLIE J. MAYER

Leslie J. Mayer is an Executive Managing Director of Retail Services for Cushman & Wakefield headquartered in Century City/Los Angeles, California. Since joining CW in 2004, she has been a key asset in the considerable growth of the Retail Platform in Southern California, domestically and cross-borders. Prior to joining Cushman & Wakefield, Leslie operated her own national retail brokerage firm, The Mayford Group for nearly 15 years.

With more than 30 years of commercial real estate experience, Ms. Mayer provides strategic planning and real-estate services to a select group of private and institutional clients, both Landlord and Tenant on regional, national, and international levels and provides leasing, sales and consulting services for restaurants, shopping centers, retail/entertainment projects, creative office buildings, and new developments. She helps tailor and develop overall market strategies for both tenants and developers as well as the acquisition, re-purposing and disposition of assets. She advises on the incubation of new retail, entertainment and restaurant concepts and spearheading their expansion programs. She has been the exclusive National Master Broker for Skechers Shoes (NYSE: SKX) for over twenty-one years.

Leslie has been recognized for her outstanding performance through a variety of awards including: Women of Achievement Century City 2022, Cushman & Wakefield Chairman's Circle Cushman & Wakefield Top 10 National Retail Broker Cushman & Wakefield Top Retail Broker of the Year, Southern California, Cushman & Wakefield President's Circle Citation Los Angeles Business Journal Winner Top Retail Transaction of the Year ,Real Estate Forum Magazine Most Powerful Women of Southern California Designee ,Real Estate Forum's Women of Influence: California and Bisnow's LA's Top Retail Broker.

To balance out her professional activities, she is actively involved in the following philanthropies and business groups: Board Member Habitat For Humanity Los Angeles Chapter, Member, USC Gould School of Law Real Estate Law and Business Forum Member, UCLA

REAG Endowment Circle/Mentor Member and as a Board Member for the Century City Chamber of Commerce.

HEATHER McCLURE

Company: Walker & Dunlop

Years in Commercial Real Estate: 25

How did you get started in commercial real estate and what age?

I started in commercial real estate at 25, two years after graduating from Texas A&M with degrees in Accounting and Latin American Studies. After working in internal audit for an international oil & gas for two years and spending two months in Lagos, Nigeria in the midst of political unrest, I concluded that a) I did not like being on the expense side ledger b) oil and gas did not excite me and c) I was tired of traveling full time.

While in Nigeria, I sent out an e-mail to my college friends and acquaintances asking them to share my resume to any groups hiring finance and accounting jobs. My Pi Beta Phi sorority sister working at Goldman Sachs in New York knew that Goldman was building out their commercial real estate group in Dallas and sent my resume to Archon's recruiter. I was fortunate that Archon hired several analyst classes while I was there, giving me exposure to new people and ideas.

At 25, I fell in love with how tangible real estate was and how I could understand the impact of the numbers on the asset itself. I immediately saw how real estate would allow me to use both qualitative and quantitative skills and how I could leverage my accounting degree to work with real assets.

Do you have an industry specialty or niche?

I specialize in financing commercial real estate developments, value-add acquisitions, and aggregations of stabilized assets. I historically have focused on debt capitalization but transitioned to equity capitalization three years ago. We identify single active LP investors, co-GP investors, and platform level investors as well as stretch seniors and preferred equity.

What advice do you have for someone entering the commercial real estate industry?

Do not be afraid to ask questions, especially when you get started. People expect you to ask questions, and when you ask clarifying questions after doing your own research first, you have already gone a long way toward earning respect. My current analyst often watches a YouTube video on unfamiliar concepts and then comes in to discuss. The habit of asking questions is critical throughout your career. Highlighting the importance of clarifying questions, I recently learned that different terms mean different things to different people in the development world. Some terms, such as "fully entitled," can be thrown around more loosely than one would expect. I think close to "shovel ready" when I hear fully entitled, and some people use that term when the site can be developed by "right" according to zoning ordinances. There is quite a disparity in timeline between those two definitions. Now, when I hear "fully entitled", I always joke and ask what exactly that means to them.

Did/do you have a mentor and how did you find him or her?

I have had a couple of mentors throughout my career. My first mentor came through my MBA program. The Real Estate Finance and Investment Center at University of Texas introduced me to my first mentor in real estate as well as a number of other seasoned professionals who had open door policies for networking and informational sessions. My second mentor was the CEO on a fund on which I was working. I did the VP to C-Suite program through CREW while working with him, and he took an active interest in my career. He was a tough negotiator and excelled at turn around situations, so he worked with me on mapping my career and refining my executive presence.

What is the best advice you have received?

When asked a question to which you do not know the answer, in most instances, you should respond "I do not know but I will find out and get back to you." Also, do not apologize unless of course you have done something for which an apology is warranted. Saying, "sorry it took so long to get back to you" weakens your position versus saying "thank you for your patience." Small changes in communication style can greatly impact others' perceptions of your capabilities.

What are three skills you need to be in the industry?

There are so many types of roles in the commercial real estate industry that allow people with different skill sets to succeed. Real estate finance requires a mix of financial acumen, written communication, and relationship skills. The ability to read a financial statement or review an underwriting model for incorrect assumptions is important for brokerage, especially raising equity. Written communication provides the opportunity to distill the key points of a deal and generate enough interest to determine whether it could be a fit for an investor. Relationship skills are critical throughout – to identify clients, to gather market information, to connect with equity sources, etc. Finally, although not a skill, curiosity is an exceptionally useful trait – be curious, be that design, people, industries, demographics, city planning, etc.

What failure stands out for you and what did you learn?

After working as a lender and borrower, I failed at transitioning to mortgage brokerage. I thought my experience structuring and negotiating loans as a lender paired with my experience on the sponsorship side would uniquely position me in the market. There are very few female mortgage bankers, and I was convinced that while it might take longer to develop a book a business, my clients would be stickier. While that may be true, I was not prepared for the internal dynamics of a mortgage brokerage shop, which resulted in as much internal competition for the right to call on clients as external competition with other brokerage shops. I ended up feeling like an island within a large organization with little internal connection. Fortunately, I verbalized my challenges and frustrations, and W&D's president and my chief production officer both understood how critical a team can be to success, especially my success. By failing as a lone mortgage banker, I had the opportunity to transition to my current role, partnering with another broker who had come from the ownership side as well to focus on equity. My partner is one of the most intelligent, knowledgeable people with whom I have worked, and we complement one another well. We raise single limited partner joint venture equity for developments and acquisition strategies Fortunately, we worked on several build-for-rent residential strategies during the earliest days of that emerging sector, so we had the opportunity to establish ourselves as experts. My failure to combine my prior experiences into mortgage banking success opened the door for me to move in a different direction, to grow, to learn more about equity and development than I could have ever imagined, and to become much better positioned to invest on my own.

What are the steps you have taken to succeed in commercial real estate?

I went back to graduate school at University of Texas's McCombs School of Business to study real estate finance. Not only did grad school allow me to learn more about finance and real estate in general, but it also gave me an incredible network of classmates and alumni with whom to network. I also have remained curious, loving to learn new strategies, explore new product types, and meet new people. Commercial real estate may be one of the easiest industries in which to network.

What question are you asked the most?

My clients often joke and ask, "when can we fund?" as soon as we complete an investment package. Raising capital is time consuming, and doing all the up-front work of vetting the proformas and putting together a marketing package can take weeks or even months if there are a number of moving pieces. After the package is complete, the real work of selling the opportunity to an investor begins, and in today's market, investors have a number of opportunities from which to choose.

What are the greatest challenges you have faced in the industry?

At the beginning of my career, the greatest challenge I faced was finding women in leadership positions. CREW Dallas at the time required six years of experience, so I did not have that as a resource. Fortunately, CREW now offers much earlier opportunities for involvement. I have seen more women enter the space, but currently my greatest challenge is coming to terms with the slow pace of change.

There are plenty of days in which I am still the only woman in the room, on the call, or in the deal. Women have a tremendous amount to offer real estate; we just need to figure out how to get women involved and interested earlier.

What is the best negotiation tip you have learned?

I have had the most success starting negotiations from a place of common ground, assuming both sides want to work together to get the deal done. I also believe having a strong real estate attorney is critical – someone who points out the risks with various business decisions but ultimately leaves the decision to you. Good counsel has enabled me to articulate concerns to the other side and come up with a win-win solution. If you are negotiating against a shark, though, mirror their tone if they do not respond favorably to de-escalation.

What time management tools or skills do you use?

Every morning, I make a list titled "Focus" to capture the deals that need my focus that day. In the past, I would title it "To Do" but since equity deals can take months, it felt defeating to not be able to mark things off the list quickly. Highlighting items on which to focus puts me in the correct mindset. Additionally, I keep my calendar updated with important family and life obligations as well business meetings. I have to create deadlines to hold myself accountable, so setting up client call check-in ensures deals do not slip through the cracks.

What advice would you give to the next generation of female leaders?

Find people with whom to network early on in your career. They can become lifelong friends. It is also critical to express an interest in investing to your counterparts, both male and female, so that you see the opportunities that arise throughout your career. Few of my female counterparts have been asked to invest regularly in deals, while my male counterparts had opportunities arise at much younger ages.

What organizations or groups do you recommend becoming part of your network?

I am very active in the University of Texas Real Estate Finance and Investment Center, and I believe some of my best relationships have come from my long-term involvement in that organization. Many universities are rolling out similar programs, so I would encourage people to reach out in their markets to the universities to see what programs they have. Depending on the market, ULI can also be an excellent network, especially WLI, CREW, NAOIP, NMHC, and Mortgage Banking Association all provide excellent resources and opportunities to network.

Looking back, what is one thing you wish you knew at the beginning of your career?

The one thing I wish I had known was that as consumers of real estate, many women innately have a sense of good real estate, good locations, and good markets. We know where we like to shop, live, work, and play. If we pay attention to those trends, we are already a step ahead. I wish I had had the nerve to invest earlier in my career and had trusted my instincts on burgeoning submarkets or strategies.

BIO - HEATHER McCLURE

Heather McClure is responsible for nationwide structured finance executions on multifamily, single-family build-to-rent, industrial, retail, office, and hospitality properties at Walker & Dunlop.

Prior to joining Walker & Dunlop, Ms. McClure was Senior Vice President of Capital Markets at Behringer, an investment management firm. There, she structured, executed, and managed $1.9 billion in debt financings on 14,000 apartment units, 1,000,000 SF of office space, a large iconic hotel with mixed use, and foreign industrial and retail. Earlier in her career, she worked for PGIM and Goldman Sachs as an originator and underwriter respectively.

Ms. McClure serves as the Co-Chair of the Advisory Council for the Real Estate Finance and Investment Center at University of Texas. She also sits on the McCombs School of Business Foundation Board.

Mollie Mossman, CPA, CMA, MBA, CRE Broker

Company: Future World Real Estate

Years in Commercial Real Estate: 30+

How did you get started in commercial real estate and what age?

I began my career with an undergraduate BBA degree and a major in accounting. Initially, I audited companies in various industries while working for a national public accounting firm. Of the different businesses I encountered, I found commercial real estate - and particularly real estate development - fascinating. I saw that it involved an orchestration of a wide variety of talents, some artistic vision and a whole lot of perseverance to take a tract of land (which we often casually refer to as "piece of dirt") and turn it into a functioning building that was also economically successful. And, if it could also involve some aesthetically pleasing architecture, then it would be a work of art for generations to enjoy inside and out!

My father had said that he thought being an auditor was a bit parasitic, because my job only existed because of a corporation that needed audit services to verify that the financial information they were presenting to the public was mostly accurate. So, I thought that being a part of the team that was creating a new silhouette on the skyline would be a whole lot more rewarding!

I also found that I preferred commercial real estate to residential. It kept weekends free for a young gal to have a big time in "Big D" (Dallas), and it also involved more discipline regarding numbers. I found I could interface well by bridging the gap between visionary entrepreneurial developers and regulated, trained-to-say-no lenders who would need to underwrite the project and be comfortable enough to invest the bank's funds in it. Presenting the economics of commercial real estate projects suited me better than the sometimes emotional realm of residential real estate, which often involves individual taste and family dynamics in selecting the right property.

I was fortunate to move from public accounting into one of the best-known Dallas development firms, Trammell Crow Company. While still in the financial area as a division controller, I kept up with development projects in the local market and soon joined a smaller developer where I could have a larger impact on the product, not just its financial aspects. In one instance, I was even able to have a pivotal role in the design of more than $100-million-dollar mixed use project, and I also obtained the commitment for its construction loan!

Do you have an industry specialty or niche?

Currently, I am interested in putting deals together using my finance, networking, research and tax expertise to deliver outsized results. This also includes brokerage services. I would also enjoy helping women developers and local women owned businesses both personally, and through my non-profit organization, Future-World Institute.

In my most recent employment position, I focused on family office commercial real estate. At this point in my career, I can almost single handedly offer a full spectrum of services to plan, analyze, manage and execute on the entire range of the family's goals for their Commercial Real Estate ("CRE"). Family offices are typically small and rarely have the ability to hire broad, in-house talent. I can offer a "cafeteria plan" of portfolio strategy, brokerage, treasury, finance and accounting as well as liaise effectively with estate planners, tax experts, and attorneys. And, when art and philanthropy are added to the CRE mix, there are some stunning finance and tax opportunities that even sophisticated family offices are often unaware of!

As both a CRE Broker and a CPA with an MBA and minor in CRE Finance, I have broad experience in various segments. I have done a lot in CRE office development and have been a CFO for a national developer of medical office and outpatient buildings. I've bought, financed, and sold mini warehouses. I have been the real estate director for a company that owned over a million square feet of manufacturing and industrial buildings as well as over 5,000 acres of land in pre-development. In 2016 I had the #2 land deal in DFW. I have been a broker on properties for several family holdings and worked on CRE deals as needed while in other positions. I brought opportunistic deal making to a national warehouse tenant that had over 500 locations in 43 states. I have been a global director of taxation and a CRE strategist at an executive level.

What advice do you have for someone entering the commercial real estate industry?

If you want to work on the transaction side, start in CRE leasing. You only have to deal with existing property. If the space is already finished out, it is just a quick make-ready for the next tenant, especially in office space. Since industrial real estate is currently a hot sector, there are good opportunities here as well, since not too many women work in that area.

Also, take whatever skills you already have and see how they might fit into CRE. If you have IT skills, there is a lot of activity in the property technology ("PropTech") space. If you like architecture, consider joining a well-established firm with a history of promoting women. If you are a lawyer, get some good experience with a firm that will qualify you to partner with someone on CRE deals later.

I was an accountant in a CPA firm and- worked my way to VP finance and then CFO of a national CRE development company. I zig-zagged into an internet Technology company and then came back to CRE as a national lease director. Then, I jumped to the family office sector and became director of real estate. My point here is to encourage you to embrace changing roles. I believe there are many interesting facets to this industry to explore. The more of them you understand, the better able you'll be to function in a pivotal role in any position you hold.

Did/do you have a mentor and how did you find him or her?

Unfortunately, only now in the very late part of my career, do I have what I would call a mentor. It happened totally organically, and I did not seek this person out.

If you have clear goals and you are comfortable telling people about them, then as you network, you may find people who want to help you achieve them, especially as more women and more women enter the industry. There is now a far greater focus on "mindful mentoring." And, industry organizations have many new programs and initiatives that did not exist until recently.

On the mentee side, I have always done the best I could to promote women I worked with, or that are part of my network and have kept them "top of mind" whenever I heard of an opening for services or employees.

What is the best advice you have received?

Let us consider that the best advice you ever receive …is the advice you put into action! I have probably received a lot of good advice that I did not note or take to heart and that may have led me down a different path, but that is in the past. Going forward, can we all be more open to others' advice and perceptions, and give them a fuller consideration? Of course! And it probably wouldn't hurt to solicit advice, which I rarely did, but probably could have benefited from.

Personally, the best CRE advice I ever received was from the top woman in commercial real estate development in Dallas, Texas - Lucy Billingsley. She is the only daughter of Trammell Crow who built a huge eponymous CRE organization. Lucy built an impressive CRE empire on her own (credit also to her husband who is a land development genius). She counseled me to "stick to my knitting", meaning to keep on doing what you're already good at. This is a more challenging directive to me than it might be to others because I am so driven to come up with new ideas, am curious about so many things and am always "up for a new challenge." Were there such a thing as an "ease of distraction index," mine would no doubt be very high!

What are three skills you need to be in the industry?

➢ **Problem** - Solving through critical thinking - eliminate things that do not matter, find the weakest links and bottlenecks, and then focus on those almost obsessively (OK I admit to being obsessive!) until resolved.

➢ **Perseverance** - the best may occasionally rest, but they're going "full out" most of the time!

➢ **Creativity** - start small. Take a new way to work. Turn things upside down or in reverse order. Build and nurture your creative skills. Decide you love all things new. Challenge yourself to come up with a new idea, no matter how initially impossible or impractical it may seem.

What failure stands out for you and what did you learn?

I thought I could easily master investing in the stock market and day trading. I lost money, and for a while, my confidence. It was considerably more shameful for me, because I am a CPA, someone people look to for financial advice.

Of course, people spend a lifetime (Warren Buffett for example) figuring out how to invest. So, why did I think I could master it on a few evenings or a few hours on the weekend? My logic is usually better than this, but it failed me for a while.

I have learned to respect the professionals in this field, and just as I would not operate on myself, stock market investments are about finding good financial services expertise. It's probably not best to invest one's own funds unless that investment offers nearly near zero risk. However, lately, thanks to the Federal Reserve Bank raising interest rates, those near zero risk assets are looking better than they have in a long time! Unfortunately, that will result in some repricing of CRE assets.

What are the steps you have taken to succeed in commercial real estate?

Key to my personal success is that I have somewhat ignored whatever title or slot I came into a company with. I have challenged myself to think like an "intrapreneur," functioning within the structure of the existing organization while pushing to help accomplish the top goals. For example, I came into a company with the title of "national lease administrator" and could have just renewed existing lease terms as my predecessor did, but within 7 months I had put an additional million dollars of net income on the bottom line by spotting opportunities and negotiating better lease terms.

I have also always worked hard and been driven to finish important tasks. This seems even more important today in a world of sound bites and endless distractions like texting, phones pinging at all hours, internet click bait and social media.

Next, they say that success is "when preparation meets opportunity." I have always kept up on reading general business publications and particularly those related to commercial real estate news. That preparation of constant reading has set me up to offer creative ideas and new inventive combinations of existing strategies put together in a new way.

Taking initiative and putting ideas into action have put me ahead of the pack on more than one occasion. Secret tip: pick up the phone and call!! There is nothing like the enthusiasm in a human voice to persuade others to help you achieve your goals. And when you smile while on the phone, it can be "heard" at the other end! Then follow up with meetings to make things happen.

Finally, I have worked hard and gotten back up when knocked down. I have persevered and mustered the grit it takes to get to the finish line.

What question are you asked the most?

Do you have this in my size? For whatever reason, when I am shopping, people think I work there!

In commercial real estate, I have held so many positions that the questions have often depended on the context and the endeavor. One thing that I am frequently asked about is "how to evaluate different strategic options." I can turn most issues into spreadsheet analyses and transform subjective issues into objective ones that are more easily understood. This is another example of bringing financial skills together with tax, critical thinking, and creativity…and continued fascination with the CRE industry!

In one position, we needed to decide which office buildings to actually develop and focus our limited resources on. We were in two dozen markets doing preliminary consulting work at any one time, so it was challenging to figure out which projects would have the highest feasibility as well as profitability. I worked with a development team from all over the country to develop a questionnaire that ranked non-quantifiable factors on a scale of 1 to 10, ranked them in importance, and then presented them in an executive summary. This led to better discussions and decisions because we had included probability of it happening, timing to completion, zoning, and "hassle factors." These critical subjective elements would otherwise have been left out and we would have only considered how much profit each one could make.

What are the greatest challenges you have faced in the industry?

Because I have been mostly in finance (on the borrower side), brokerage and development, the greatest and also most surprising challenge has been the extent to which CRE is male dominated, particularly in privately held companies. Or, perhaps I should say that women are still not getting the promotions and opportunities they should. The surprising part is the extent to which this challenge still exists today, nearly 40 years later.

During a rant at my hairdressers (and after 30 plus years, this person is family!) about yet another discriminatory situation in the work place, I was asked "why did you go into commercial real estate in the first place and then stay?" I answered that "I thought it would change!" I hope I have been a part of that change. I would like others like me, who have also made these "maiden voyages" to leave a large wake for those that follow after us, helping along the way.

Now let's take a moment to highlight that things have gotten better. Particularly in the banking world, there has been marked improvement. For example, Richard Fisher - when he chaired the Dallas Federal Reserve Bank - groomed a crop of talented women there and we now see more women leaders throughout the banking system.

And of course, all the "gross stuff" is gone. If you are interested in what I am talking about, then just ask any women my age and we'll regale you with stories that now would put the perpetrators out on their ear, out on the street, or into a court room.

What is the best negotiation tip you have learned?

Never underestimate the power of the "take-away!" So much of Commercial Real Estate success is timing. If you can walk away from something and the other party does not have that luxury, it gives you tremendous leverage. And sometimes it can also be an effective bluff - if you are willing to take that risk.

Remember that negotiation is not fighting, it is communication. You propose something and someone responds. That response can contain a lot more information in it than just the overt meaning. Look for the nuances in the response and ask some good questions about the underlying implications.

Of course, the most rewarding negotiations are ideally the win-win variety, but sometimes you are in a weak position and you just have to do the best you can.

Finally, have you noticed that the big lease deals you read about in the CRE news are usually negotiated by 2 or more people on each side? Do not negotiate alone if you do not have to. If you are the owner, get representation - if you are the tenant or buyer, it will not usually cost anything because your CRE broker will get paid by splitting the Seller's Broker's commission. And, even if you do have some cost, another experienced CRE mind will more than pay for itself and most likely bring up many things you would not have considered until you find out you have overlooked a problem months or years later.

I see that the request in this section as for "just one tip," but after today I would like to add one more. I was at an in-person meeting while representing a woman CRE owner. I was struck with the advantage men have when they meet in person. They are generally bigger, talk louder, and often use dominant body language. This is OK as long as you don't agree to too much at the meeting and redirect the negotiations back to subsequent emails, phone calls and documents. It is on the phone and through remote communication that I believe women are on more equal footing and even may have an edge. In the depths of a CRE downturn, I called over 50 lenders and could only get two quotes. I heavily negotiated the loan terms on the phone with a lender in Boston. He must have envisioned I was "an Amazon," because when he came to Dallas to close the loan, he admonished himself for having given so may deal points away to "a little blonde gal!"

What time management tools or skills do you use?

I like deadlines and will self-impose them to help motivate myself to complete tasks. For example, when I was a VP of Finance, responsible for obtaining CRE development and/or permanent or acquisition financing for office buildings, I would set an appointment with a local lender I knew well, even if the deal was not going to fit their underwriting standards. That meeting would be my self-imposed deadline to have the loan package completed.

In most of my positions, I have often managed short- and long-term projects simultaneously. Each project had varying degrees of importance. Various tasks can often be for different owners. And, sometimes things are "everything, everywhere all at once!" This requires an ability to multi-task and change priorities quickly. If this is something you can already do, you will have an edge in accepting all the changes that will inevitably take place over a long project, and still stay on track.

I sometimes postpone taking action and send some particularly challenging problem to my subconscious. It's amazing the things you'll think of while gardening, driving or doing something else totally unrelated.

I also make it a priority to set aside time to read industry publications and the local news. This pays dividends over time to understand how different companies handle decisions. You can better expand your network by being able to converse about other people's projects and suggest ways you might help each other.

Finally, I find lists exhausting. I can seemingly make endless lists. And, sometimes they get overwhelming. So, selecting the top three priorities from your to do list each week works better for me than lengthy lists that include many other lesser priority items.

What advice would you give to the next generation of female leaders?

First, let me say how exciting it is to be offering guidance to future a female leader!! I hope there will be many of you. Our primary purpose in writing this book is to empower you and let you know that you are already enjoying a hard-won path toward success in CRE, one that all of us will continue to support and widen. Seek out firms that are led by women and "enlightened" men, or firms that already have women in the C-suite.

If you are not finding those opportunities, see if you can find out if the CEO, and/or #2 person, such as the EVP and/or the owners have daughters that are of working age. If you work for men who have only sons, they may only see themselves in other young men and may not be able to visualize themselves promoting you or seeing you as a leader. Or, possibly their wife, sister or mother work in a profession? If not, perhaps you can have a discussion around diversity (which was not possible "back in the day"!) I remember interviewing for a national CFO job and was concerned because the CEO had only sons and a non-working wife. But the EVP had two working daughters and he pushed for me to be hired. The corporate culture was good there until he left the company.

Ask for help. I was often so reluctant to do so. I have an affinity for research and can often get into deep searches that can run very late at night on the internet. I have tried to figure too many things out myself. You can often do better by leaving enough time to ping your network or contact someone new. Sometimes it is not best to be the smartest person in the room, but rather the person who got the most sleep! That way you can present ideas and stimulate discussions rather than having "all the answers" but be sleep-deprived and unable to function at your best.

Next, do not be afraid to jump to a new company for a better opportunity. It was initially very hard to get promoted within a CRE company, so I would master the existing job and deliver exceptional results. But then, if there was nowhere for me to move up, I'd take the initiative to look for the next rung up at a different firm and was able to move up considerably faster than trying to climb the rungs where I was.

Finally, develop external power - attend events, write articles, get known for what you are doing, especially if that is not happening where you work now. I got in trouble once for giving a lecture at a bank. But then, when a local university also wanted me to speak, my boss changed his attitude and was more supportive, due to this outside recognition.

What organizations or groups do you recommend becoming part of your network?

Try out different groups and see where you find a comfortable fit for you – do not automatically assume they will not be helpful. Because I had so much office experience, I almost passed up becoming a part of IAMC, the Industrial Asset Management Council, the leading professional association for corporate real estate executives who are focused on the needs of an industrial portfolio. IAMC is good at helping build valuable relationships.

I have also enjoyed ULI - Urban Land Institute, REFEA -Real Estate Finance Executives Association, and CREW - Commercial Real Estate Women - which gets better every year. I've also been in organizations for CPAs and CMAs (Certified Management Accountants) due to my multiple professional licenses.

Early on, I did not join groups that are for women only. I felt that separate was not equal. And, I felt that my time was too limited to not be "in the room" with decision makers. I wanted to have at least some facetime and a brief introduction (particularly since I was working nearly twice as hard as my male counterparts ...and I was still somehow supposed to find time for shopping and dating!). Decades ago, I usually had to do self-introductions anytime I could - even in the coffee line. Some of this was because there was a technique that I first witnessed at Trammel Crow, where groups of men would stand shoulder to shoulder in a circle to deliberately block others from joining. If you tapped someone in the circle on the shoulder, they would ignore you or turn around, keeping the circle intact, and direct you elsewhere.

But this has changed, and women in professional groups can help you a great deal since women have achieved so much now and hold more powerful roles. Just remember to respect their time – you know how hard these gals worked to get there!

Looking back, what is one thing you wish you knew at the beginning of your career?

Commercial Real Estate has (sometimes vicious) business cycles. I started right before the big downturn in the mid-eighties. So even though I got some small, limited partnership interests, they quickly became worthless in the subsequent CRE crash. But I was extremely glad I had been a limited and not a general partner who was financially liable!

That tumultuous time made me forever shy away from taking deal positions again. I stuck to working for salaries with performance-based bonuses. I also took a decade and worked in Internet technology - and guess what? In the early 2000s, I found out that other industries could have crashes as well!

However, that means I missed the super expansionary times for CRE, and I wish I had not. If you can get an equity stake in deals through ownership, partnership, or vesting, it can produce long term cash-flow and net worth that will build wealth that you can comfortably retire on.

BIO - Mollie Mossman

Mollie Mossman CPA, CMA, MBA, CRE Broker, is a veteran commercial real estate ("CRE") executive with additional experience in internet technology and the accelerator/start up community. She has created unique "overlay" portfolio strategies for corporate and prominent families' extensive real estate holdings, as well as financed and/or brokered hundreds of millions of dollars worth of property. She was a CFO for a national developer of medical offices and outpatient healthcare facilities and has managed in-person and remote teams.

Active in several CRE national and local organizations, she has been a guest lecturer at the University of North Texas, Bank of America, and Urban Land Institute. As a past board member of an accelerator/start-up non-profit organization, she continues to be enthusiastic about "what comes next" in CRE and enjoys helping new companies succeed.

Mollie lives in the Dallas area with her flock, which includes her husband and a very spunky parrot.

AMY PJETROVIC

Company: Venture Commercial Real Estate

Years in Commercial Real Estate: 17

How did you get started in commercial real estate and what age?

I was 23 years old when I stumbled on commercial real estate. I was working on my masters in college and working at my parent's restaurant while trying to figure out what I wanted to do next. I had never thought about retail brokerage as a career. One of our customers at the restaurant happened to head up Venture's graphics department and he asked me to come and help out with some basic data entry for the company website and I decided to do it. I was at the company for a few months and while there I had the opportunity to gain a better understanding about retail brokerage. I loved it. Something in my gut was telling me this is the path for me and that I could be successful doing it! I asked the company for an internship and they took a chance on me and today…17 years later I am one of three Principal owners of the firm. I was the first woman to ever make Partner.

Do you have an industry specialty or niche?

Venture is a Retail firm and I specialize in Landlord and Seller representation. When I first began my career, I did a mixture of tenant representation and Landlord representation but early on I decided to intentionally and exclusively focus on the Landlord side. Initially, it was challenging to have the discipline to turn down tenant representation assignments, but I felt it would deter me from working as hard as I could and being the greatest advocate for all my landlord clients. I realized whenever I had a tenant representation meeting or market tour that I needed to prepare for it would cause my landlord listings to get put on hold while I prepared for my tenant meeting. From my perspective, I felt I was doing a good job doing both tenant representation and Landlord representation, but I decided I wanted to specialize on one side so that I could do an EXCELLENT job for my clients. I wanted to feel truly confident that my clients were getting the absolute best service and that I was adding as much value as I could.

What advice do you have for someone entering the commercial real estate industry?

Find a great mentor. This business can be intimidating in the beginning and having guidance from someone who has been through it is invaluable. Find advocates within your company. Develop and continue to strengthen the relationships within your peer group since you will come up together and become valuable sources to one another. Put in the work and the extra effort….it will pay off.

Did/do you have a mentor and how did you find him or her?

I have had a business mentor for about 8 years now and he was introduced to me through one of the other Principals at Venture. This mentor has really helped guide me to becoming a better leader and a stronger broker. In some instances, it has been as simple as he gives me assurance and confidence to know that I can push myself to the next level. We have weekly calls for about 30 minutes. In another instance we dissected my working deals and decided I would not list anything smaller than a certain size. He has been someone that I can bounce ideas off when I might feel uncertain. He also helps keep me accountable and that accountability goes a long way!

What is the best advice you have received?

Do what it takes to become an expert in the area of real estate you are dedicating yourself to.

What are three skills you need to be in the industry?

➤ You need to be a good communicator

➤ Good listener

➤ Persistence

What failure stands out for you and what did you learn?

My failure was leasing a small 1500 sf space in a strip center out in the suburbs during the downturn in 2009/2010. I just could not get this small space leased and the building was owned by an individual (husband and wife) that really hadn't had much experience in CRE. They called me so often and criticized my efforts and constantly said I wasn't doing enough. I was so young and had no long term or big picture perspective yet and I let this one experience start affecting my confidence. I took two lessons away from this failure. The first lesson was that it takes expertise to differentiate and articulates that, in some instances, it could actually take years to lease a difficult vacancy. The second lesson was that time is all we have and we need to determine whether the time spent is worthwhile.

What are the steps you have taken to succeed in commercial real estate?

I defined an area of CRE that I wanted to specialize in and then became an expert in this area. I soaked up as much information as I could whenever I could. I set annual goals. I consistently asked mentors, clients and senior brokers for feedback and what I can improve upon so that I could continue to grow and challenge myself.

What question are you asked the most?

"How do you manage all your listings and working deals?"

I have tried different organizational tools over the years and one simple thing I always do is track every single deal I have working on a spreadsheet. I stay very committed to doing this. I typically run through this active deal report once per week to make sure things are on track and nothing is falling through the cracks. In addition to this, and depending on each client's particular needs, I create simple activity reports (usually just in excel or word) for each project so that we can track prospective tenants or buyers and update our clients accordingly. At the current time I have 40 listings and many of these listings are substantial in size meaning hundreds of acres or several hundred thousand square feet of retail for lease. I also have a small team I work with to manage all these listings and having the right team in place makes it easier to successfully manage a large portfolio of properties. There is no doubt when you have the right team in place it makes each day more enjoyable. When you have dependable team members to work with it makes the disappointments a little easier and it sure makes the successes more fun!

What are the greatest challenges you have faced in the industry?

In the beginning, it was a challenge to trust my intuition, not doubt and second guess myself. I had to gain my confidence, find my voice and learn to trust my expertise and knowledge. The more you intentionally do this the easier and more second nature it becomes and you begin to grow and each success leads to a stronger voice and greater confidence.

When things get more challenging and more problem solving is required it will oftentimes necessitate giving more of your time with much less of a return. The challenging times are when you can help to add value and build relationships. It is easy when the economy is great and deals are abundant but people remember when you added value and helped when times were difficult.

What is the best negotiation tip you have learned?

Get on the phone and have a discussion (rather than an email or a text message).

What time management tools or skills do you use?

I track all my working deals in a spreadsheet and this allows me to understand my current and future pipeline and keeps me organized and efficient. Time blocking also helps make sure you are allocating the necessary and appropriate amount of time towards each project. I also manage my time by finding the right team members and making sure I am delegating the appropriate assignments or tasks. Over the years I have found that loyalty is a two-way street and you need to take care of your team. It can be time consuming and challenging to train and develop a new team member that you can entrust with your clients and projects so when you have the right team in place do your best to take care of them.

What advice would you give to the next generation of female leaders?

Find an organization with competent caring leadership and a successful senior person you can learn from and helps you grow in the business.

What organizations or groups do you recommend becoming part of your network?

Try different groups till you find one that you enjoy. NTCAR, TREC, CREW. Some groups may feel more like a chore but when you find the right one it can become a place where you build friendships and find opportunities.

Looking back, what is one thing you wish you knew at the beginning of your career?

I wish I knew how valuable it would be to have a mentor that looks out for your best interest and can help guide you through uncertainties.

BIO - AMY PJETROVIC

Amy is one of three Principal owners at Venture Commercial Real Estate and has more than 17 years of retail leasing and sales experience. Amy's specialization is seller and Landlord representation. She has always believed in the importance of functioning as a team with her clients, treating their goals and objectives as though they were her own in order to add value and achieve the best possible outcome for each client.

Amy has closed more than 600 lease/sale transactions and has represented some of the same clients since starting in the business over 17 years ago. She is consistently a top producer at the firm.

Amy's passion for Commercial Real Estate has developed into a broad experience level that includes development and implementation of leasing and sales strategies where she analyzes, negotiates and executes transactions for her clients. Her listing experience includes retail developments with a focus on mixed use and grocery anchored shopping centers.

She has listed, advised and helped merchandise and plan for land parcels ranging from less than 1 acre to over hundreds of acres. Amy holds her CCIM certification, was recognized in 2018's Women in Real Estate Forum and is annually recognized as a D CEO Top Retail Power Broker.

She is an active member of International Council of Shopping Centers, Deals in Heels and is an active Board Member with North Texas Commercial Association of Realtors.

HEATHER PRICHARD

Company: Ziglar Realty

Years in Commercial Real Estate: 22

How did you get started in commercial real estate and what age?

I am going into my 22nd year as a full-time real estate salesperson. I got my licenses when I was 26 years old. I did not feel young at the time, but I look back now and realize how grateful I was to be involved in this business as a young woman. I now have the privilege to sponsor several agents in their young 20's. It is so exciting to see the next generation coming into the real estate industry.

I took a position to manage a real estate office and quickly got the "fire in my belly" to sell real estate. Every payday I saved money to buy my next real estate course. It took me about 4-6 months to complete the courses, but after I passed my exam, I went into sales full time. I was a single mom at the time. I remember the first day I sat at my desk as a commission only salesperson. I had a talk with myself. I said, "Success isn't an option, it's a necessity and you have to make this work." I immediately dug my high heels in and got to work!

The mentor I worked for at the time taught me to show up for my business every single day! To this day, I am grateful for her teaching me that habit. I take days off for family time and personal growth, but to this day I still show up for my business full time, everyday!

I have spent over half of my career specializing in commercial real estate. I think it is so important to pick a niche that you have a passion for. I still sell other types of real estate including some residential and farm and ranch, but my specialty is commercial sales. I have built a reputation in my community as the 'go to' commercial real estate agent and I carry that reputation close to my heart. I protect it by doing business with the upmost integrity, always putting my client best interest first, continuing to educate myself, and I put relationships before deals!

Do you have an industry specialty or niche?

I am a proud Texan and live in an area that thrives from oil and gas related economics. Considering this, I specialize in Industrial Real Estate Sales.

When I decided commercial real estate what I wanted to specialize in, I started attending every training event and read every book could get my hands on. I also work with clients who invest in land development, multi-family, and retail. Industrial commercial real estate has been and continues to be my primary sales.

I have had the honor to work with the most respected oil and gas companies on the globe and grateful to have represented many of them as Sellers and Buyers. It is not the niche I expected to specialize in, but my husband and I would not trade it for anything. He joined me full time in our real estate company about 6 years ago. We are living our dream working together and we both primarily work with industrial real estate clients. I think it is important to learn all aspects of real estate, but having a niche makes you the respected professional in your community for that industry.

What advice do you have for someone entering the commercial real estate industry?

My best advice to someone getting into the commercial real rate industry would be to hire a business coach to help you on your journey. I wish I would have hired one way earlier on and things would have gone smoother. I could have run my business more effectively. Having someone to help you create systems, checks, and balances and hold you accountable is critical. A business coach will help you streamline your business in a manner it can be scalable and grow!

The next piece of advice is to be a good boss to yourself. Do not allow yourself to not show up to do your best every day. Many times, I have seen agents go to work for themselves and only commit a few hours a week to their business. An agent must dedicate themselves and work as hard for their own business as they would for an employer. I know people who are employees of a business and show up to work 50 hours a week. They show up and dedicate themselves to building someone else's business for a paycheck. Then they get their real estate licenses, and dedication is lacking. Agents who succeed in this business commit to their business and treat it as a business. They invest time, money, and energy to build it and constantly do so for many years.

The third thing is whatever you decide to do to market yourself, be consistent. Do it every day and hold yourself accountable to do so. You must stay in front of people to stay on top of their mind. This can be done very effectively and cheap now that we have social media, but the old fashion basics still work as well. Examples of these include handwritten notecards, mailers, email, coffee with a friend, attending community events, and a good solid CRM, (customer relationship management).

Did/do you have a mentor and how did you find him or her?

I do have a several mentors. I am a Ziglar Legacy Speaker and Trainer through the Zig Ziglar Corporation. Through the certification process I met my partner with Ziglar Realty, Julie Ziglar. She is the daughter of the respected Zig Ziglar. Julie and I along with her daughter DeDe Galindo created and launched Ziglar Realty in August 2020. Together we have created an amazing company that was designed by the legacy of her father. Julie is one of my most precious mentors and friend. Julie brings light and joy everywhere she goes. She loves on people anytime they are in her presence, and she has a gift to make everyone around her to feel special. Julie is the epitome of ethics, values, and dedication. I am abundantly blessed to have her as a friend and business partner. I have grown so much as a woman and businesswoman having her in my life and as a mentor.

I also have a business coach and I met her through the Ziglar Corporation as a well. We met several years ago and having her as a mentor has helped me take things "next level." She helps me dig deep and streamline my business for growth and productivity. She also helps me create solutions for areas I am struggling through as a business owner. I would not be where I am today in my personal life or business without our weekly coaching meetings. You may question if you can afford a mentor. Honestly, your business cannot afford for you not to hire a mentor. It is a critical part of investing in business and yourself so you can achieve what your designed to accomplish without sacrificing what is most important!

What is the best advice you have received?

I was asked a simple but validated question early in my career by a mentor. As an agent in my second year of business he asked me, "Are you the top producer in your area yet?" My reply was, "Well, not yet" He responded with these very intriguing words. "I know you have the same opportunity, talent, and probably offer as good as or better service to your clients as they do. So, tell me, what are they doing that you are not?"

I never really saw myself as an equal to the top producers in the area of talent and service. Truth was, I had as much to offer the buyers and sellers in my community as any of the top five producers in my area did. I quickly took an inventory of what I was investing into my business and what systems I needed to apply to become a top producer in my area. It was not long after this, I was a top producer and continue to be to this day. When you begin to think like a top producer and believe you are one, the title will follow. You must believe in yourselves before others will believe in you.

What are three skills you need to be in the industry?

The most important skills a real estate agent needs are honesty and integrity. These two qualities will be the thing that define your reputation. You are assisting people with one of the most valuable investments many will ever make. They want to work with someone they can trust. If people trust you and like you, they will do business with you. A good reputation cannot be purchased, it can only be earned. The reputation you build in your community will stay with you throughout your entire career. I have built my business on honestly and integrity and I believe without a doubt that is why I am still successful.

The next thing I believe is an important skill to building a lasting career is self-discipline. A real estate agent is considered an independent contractor. Your broker's responsibility is to provide support and training, but you must have the self-discipline to show up for your business every morning. You can get motivation from many sources including a mentor, your broker, attending events, reading, and even your favorite podcasts, but motivation is temporary. You most have self-discipline for the days you are not feeling motivated.

Relationship building is another skill necessary for a successful career in real estate. If you are in sales, you are in a relationship business. It is imperative to be involved with the people in your community and build meaningful relationships with them. Relationships will create a long-lasting business for many years to come. When selling real estate, it is a whole customer experience. Relationships in a sales business can be summed up in these three questions.

1. What did you do to build a relationship to make your client choose you to represent them in their transaction?

2. What did you do during the transaction that will make clients remember you?

3. How will you nurture your relationships after the sale?

You must be there for your clients and impress them before, during, and after the sale. Many times, the before and after are more important than the during. What did you do during the transaction that will make clients remember you. Remember, it is about creating a whole customer experience.

What failure stands out for you and what did you learn?

A failure I learned early on in my career and an expensive mistake was in the following up! The paycheck is in the follow up! I lost a few deals early in my career due to not following up in a timely manner. If you are not willing show up when a client needs you, there is another agent willing to. I spend at least an hour a day following up on leads. If you invest in a high-level CRM, you can set up smart plans that can help you with follow up. It can also help you streamline your leads that will lead to growth in your business for many years to come.

What are the steps you have taken to succeed in commercial real estate?

Like with anything, it starts with your first deal. If you market it properly, follow up with all leads, and service them with a high level of professionalism, it will lead to the next deal. Maintaining multiple listings will keep the leads coming in and in return it creates new buyer leads and additional listings.

Perfecting the commercial contacts and addendums is critical. Get a good commercial real estate attorney to help you navigate through this process. I work with my clients' attorneys on many of our transactions. I have familiarized myself with the due diligence period and necessary documents to complete a commercial transaction effectively. I am very comfortable having extensive conversations with all our clients' attorneys during our commercial transactions. I am continually learning and growing my knowledge in the commercial real estate industry so I can best service my client's needs.

Knowledge of the commercial market and economics that drive the market are also imperative in commercial real estate.

What question are you asked the most?

"How is the market?" Is the number one question I am asked. Everywhere I go someone wants to talk real estate. I have never met anyone who is not interested in owning real estate on some level. They either already own real estate or want to know how to buy it.

Many people in the public want to know how the current economic forces are driving the current real estate market. Being educated on these topics allow me the opportunity to have an educated discussion. This opens doors to building relationships.

What are the greatest challenges you have faced in the industry?

Shifts in the market are going to happen. If you have not been in one, it is not a matter of if, but when you will. When things are "good," save your money and invest it wisely. When the market shifts, your marketing may have as well. You may have to get creative in closing deals. Many people have become millionaires in a shifting market. It is all a matter of perspective. Shifts are known for filtering out the ones who will make it in this business and the ones who will not. Stand strong and keep working hard and you will be the small percentage who makes it!

What is the best negotiation tip you have learned?

Do not be shy but be respectable. As the infamous Zig Ziglar says, "Shy salespeople have skinny kids." Strong negotiation skills require a great deal of confidence. You will find confidence from knowledge in the current market and industry. Always remember who you are representing and keep their best interest first.

What time management tools or skills do you use?

One of Zig Ziglar's famous quotes is "You must plan to win, prepare to win, and then you expect to win!" Morning routine and night routine are a must. Get up early! If you wake by 6am you can accomplish what most important before 11:00 am. My morning routine consists of making my bed, praying, journaling, reflection of the way I want the day to look, hydrate, nutrition, exercise, and get ready for success. I get dress for success every morning. I never know when my next million-dollar client will call me or when I will have an opportunity to make my next first impression. I then spend two hours checking email, updated current files, returning phone calls, following up with leads, and writing handwritten note cards. I look over my to do list and get as many things knocked out as possible, beginning with what is most important for the day. I have all these things finished by around 11:00 am. A nightly routine is just as important as a morning routine. A nightly routine consists of bedtime habits to help you relax and sleep well. One thing that helps me sleep well is a bed that I look forward to getting into each night. I have always told my kids to spend the money necessary to have a comfortable bed and cozy bedding. We spend approximately a third of our life in bed, make it comfortable at any expense. Before bed I like to take a hot shower, review my to do list for the next day and write down anything I need to brain dump. I then like to journal or read, diffuse a relaxing essential oil, and pray. This is also a time for pillow talk with my husband. Questions I ask myself at the end of the day: Did I LIVE fully? Did I LOVE fully? Did I MAKE a difference? Did I GIVE my best? It is personal life habits that will help you be successful in your professional life. We all have the same 24 hours. What are seeds are sowing today? The fruit is on the vine ready to be harvested. It is yours for the taken. You cannot expect to have a basket full if you are not willing to pick it! Every morning you are blessed with a gift... the gift of life. What kind of life you are going to choose? WHO will you CHOOSE to be a part of it? Who will you CHOOSE to be in it? WHO will you become? CHOOSE what is important because we will not get today back. We cannot buy back yesterday, and we are not promised tomorrow. Today is all we are promised, so make it count!

What advice would you give to the next generation of female leaders?

My best advice for female leaders is to lift one another up and help others on their journey. I believe God made women Wife's and Mother's because of our pure hearts and desires to cultivates an environment to cheerfully serve and build each other up. We are good stewards of our homes, time and resources. As women, we have unswerving integrity, patience, and kindness. Our strength is found in our intelligence, our dignity, our class, and our smiles. We stand together to lift one another up. When we help other women shine, our light shines brighter. To me, this describes qualities of an amazing woman and amazing real estate agent.

What organizations or groups do you recommend becoming part of your network?

One of the most beneficial groups I have been a part of is the local chamber of commerce and economic development centers (EDC). It takes time to nurture these relationships to become their "go to" commercial real estate agent, but when you do it is a great compliment. Take time to get to know the elected officials in your community as well. You will be working with them on assisting clients with permits, zoning ordinances, and future growth needs in your community. Being involved in any commercial related organizations in your area and state will be beneficial as well. I have been blessed to build cherished relationships with many respected commercial agents across Texas by being involved in commercial real estate activities and events across the state.

Looking back, what is one thing you wish you knew at the beginning of your career?

Have no fear! I have found a common factor that causes agents to fail. FEAR and EXCUSES! It is bondage!! Imagine yourself wrapped in chains. When you overcome this one thing, you can achieve anything. An excuse is nothing less than a well-planned lie! You have zero excuses! Go live out your life's destiny and accomplish what you were designed to accomplish. You are able and you all have opportunity waiting. Through the years we have been conditioned for mediocrity. Go be extra...Extra Ordinary! Skills cannot be taken from you. You have zero excuses, so go become everything you were meant to be. As Zig Ziglar would say, "Go sell something!"

BIO- HEATHER PRICHARD

Heather Prichard is an award-winning Broker with more than two decades of real estate sales experience. More than 20 years ago she received the "Rookie of the Year" award her first year in the business and opened her first office a few years later when she was 27 years old. She is currently the active Broker and Co-Owner of ZIGLAR Realty. Heather specializes in Commercial, Luxury, and Residential sales in Texas. Heather is licensed in multiple states including Texas, Oklahoma, Georgia, and Maine and will soon add Tennessee and New Mexico to her resume.

Heather has served as President of the Women's Council of Realtors two separate terms and was elected and served as President of her local Board of Realtors. She has chaired many Realtor Committees, served on the Board of Directors, and on the Agent Leadership Council. Heather currently serves on the Texas Realtors Professional and Development committee. In addition to many top producing awards, Heather was voted "Super Agent" in Texas Monthly Magazine. Heather has built her business on referrals and credits much of her success to her clients.

In addition to real estate, Heather is a Nationally Recognized and Certified Zig Ziglar Legacy Key-note Speaker, Trainer, and Coach. She is also a Certified Business and Life Coach through Ziglar Inc. She loves sharing her leadership and business skills with other professionals in the real estate industry.

When she is not working, Heather commits her free time to her family. She and her husband, Kit, have two grown children with their spouses and four grandchildren to love on and cherish.

KARA RAFFERTY

Company: Outside the Box Real Estate, The Rafferty Firm and The Office Collaborative

Years in Commercial Real Estate: 26

How did you get started in commercial real estate and what age?

I started in the commercial real estate business when I was in my late 20's. I came to the business through a move to Texas and a career change. Prior to moving to Dallas, I was a licensed attorney in Minnesota working as a prosecutor for the City of Minneapolis. When I realized I would be moving to Texas to be with my ex-husband, I was determined to make the move to retail real estate. Before I made the move, every time I would visit Dallas, I would set up a meeting with someone in retail real estate. At each of those meetings, I would ask for additional names and contacts for people in the industry. I continued to network and six months after my move, one of the people I met almost a year earlier, Sherry Koetting, hired me for my first job in retail leasing at Jones Lang Wootton which eventually became ING Clarion.

Do you have an industry specialty or niche?

I have always done retail leasing, but now I have also incorporated office leasing and law into my practice.

What advice do you have for someone entering the commercial real estate industry?

Network. Get to know as many people as you can, not just in your area of real estate, but with people from other sectors of the business. Real estate is a relationship business. It is very important that you take the time to develop your relationships.

Did/do you have a mentor and how did you find him or her?

I have had several mentors throughout my career. My first was Steve Toppel. We worked together at my first job at ING Clarion. I knew very little about retail leasing when I first started. Steve's career prior to real estate was as a teacher. He was very good at teaching me the ropes of the business. I still have notes from back then! Then when I went out on my own, Jenny Reynolds has been a great resource for me. I know Jenny from a project we both worked on in the early 2000s.

What is the best advice you have received?

Return all calls within 24 hours. Even if it is someone you do not want or need to talk with, you can always leave a message after hours or send a quick email. But ALWAYS respond. You never know where someone will end up working and relationships are the key to the real estate business.

What are three skills you need to be in the industry?

First, excellent communication, both written and oral. Most areas of real estate involve negotiations of some form. Being able to communicate your position effectively is essential.

Second, an understanding of finance. Know how to structure the economics of a deal and how to manipulate the numbers to get the required return.

Third, be good at marketing. Real estate involves selling your space or property. If you represent a tenant, then you need to sell them to the landlord in order for your tenant to get the best deal possible.

What failure stands out for you and what did you learn?

I was in New York for a convention and took some real estate people that worked at American Eagle out for dinner. We went to this fancy restaurant in mid-town. As the waiter took our order, he asked if we would like the entrée topped with truffles. We all thought that sounded good and ordered the truffle topping. I knew I was in trouble when the food came not just topped with truffles, but 14K gold shavings! I had no idea that gold was edible. The bill was outrageous! It was around $500 per person. I was so nervous to turn in that expense report. When I explained the situation to my boss, he smiled and told me a similar story that happened to him early in his career. He approved the expense but told me to not let it happen again. After that experience, I always make sure to ask what the "extras" cost before ordering.

What are the steps you have taken to succeed in commercial real estate?

My career has been primarily on the Landlord side. I have leased properties all over the country. Whenever I take on a new property, I spend a lot of time trying to understand the market.

Where is the competition, who are the active brokers, what categories are overrepresented or lacking, demographics, etc. Then I find people and publications in the market that will keep me up to date on things happening in and around the area. Doing a deep dive initially gives you direction on where to take the property and assists you in recognizing opportunities.

I have also made sure I am always learning something new. It is important to continue to grow and expand your skill set.

What question are you asked the most?

Do you have any off-market properties you are trying to sell? I get asked this question at least once a week via text and/or email. I do some foreclosure work through my law practice. That may be why I am a target for these calls.

What are the greatest challenges you have faced in the industry?

By far the hardest time for me was in 2011 after the real estate fallout from the great recession. I was working at JLL at the time as a salaried employee in their mall division. I had just been through a contentious divorce and was a single parent mom with two young children. At the beginning of the year, we had our annual meeting in Atlanta. At the meeting, they brought each of us in and told us our salaries were essentially being cut in half and we were moving to a commission-based structure. I was scared to death and didn't know how I was going to get by in an environment where not many deals were happening. However, this change ended up being more lucrative than my salaried position. JLL entered the receivership arena and obtained a lot of shopping centers that were taken over by the bank. These properties had been neglected for years and had tenants operating with expired leases. Whenever you got on a new receivership property, there was a lot of meat on the bone due to the renewals that needed to be done with the surviving tenants. For new deals, you had to get very creative in your deal structure since there was no money to give for tenant allowance. I learned and grew a lot during this challenging period of my career.

What is the best negotiation tip you have learned?

Patience. Sometimes it is better to walk away from a negotiation and let it sit for a while. It allows the parties to get away from the minutia and determine what is most important to both parties. You can re-approach the negotiation with a new perspective. The bottom line is we all just want to get the deal done.

What time management tools or skills do you use?

I still use a wire bound Franklin Daily Planner to organize my days. I wake up very early in the morning and spend time reviewing my day. I set priorities, organize my time and determine the one main thing that needs to get done. By spending time each morning planning my day, I feel I live more intentionally.

What advice would you give to the next generation of female leaders?

Take some risks and get outside your comfort zone regularly. It is how you grow as a person and in your career.

What organizations or groups do you recommend becoming part of your network?

My favorite networking group is Deals in Heels. The women writing this book are all members. It is a Dallas based group of women in the retail real estate industry. I am also a CCIM (Certified Commercial Investment Member) and active in the North Texas CCIM chapter. The CCIM designation is a great way to improve your understanding of the financial side of the real estate business. If you are in retail, then joining the ICSC (International Council of Shopping Centers) is essential. The ICSC hosts conferences, meetings, and events worldwide. Other organizations that are also worthwhile include

CREW (Commercial Real Estate Women), your local Commercial Association of Realtors and ULI (Urban Land Institute).

Looking back, what is one thing you wish you knew at the beginning of your career?

Invest in real estate as early as you can. Buy a rental house, duplex, small office, land, retail, etc. Real Estate typically appreciates in value and has a lot of tax benefits. Especially if you are a real estate professional. It is a great way to create wealth.

BIO - KARA RAFFERTY

Kara Rafferty has been in the Commercial Real Estate industry for over 25 years. She received her BS from the University of Minnesota and her Law Degree from Mitchell Hamline School of Law. Kara is a licensed real estate broker in Texas and Louisiana. She is a licensed attorney in Texas and Minnesota (inactive).

Kara also has the real estate designations of a SCLS (Senior Certified Leasing Specialist), CRX (Certified Retail Property Executive), and CCIM (Certified Commercial Investment Member). She has worked for Landlords on a variety of retail leasing projects throughout the country and most recently leased Class A Lifestyle Centers in Texas and Louisiana including Market Street The Woodlands.

She has worked on Regional Malls, Grocery Anchored Centers, Strip Centers and Net Lease Deals. Kara also has retail redevelopment, development and acquisitions experience.

TANYA RAGAN

Company: President/Owner of Wildcat Management

Years in Commercial Real Estate: 17

How did you get started in commercial real estate and what age?

I have been in commercial real estate for about 17 years. Today, I am the president and owner of Wildcat Management, a real estate development, investment, and construction company with offices throughout the United States. Our headquarters are located in downtown Dallas, Texas. We also work in Oil and Gas, and Venture Capital (early-stage companies).

I have a corporate background and spent many years in the high-paced world of New York City.

I actually started in fashion and worked for various Fortune 500 companies, including Timberland, Liz Claiborne, Oshkosh, and Neiman Marcus. I was the youngest director at a publicly traded company when I met my cap and felt I was ready to go out on my own.

I had spent years making these companies money and it was time to do it for myself.

I evaluated where my skill set would be best served and learned about opportunities in Texas, where they had the largest natural gas discovery in North America called the Barnett Shale. I had experience managing fractionalized family interests in minerals throughout North Dakota, so I knew a thing or two about oil and gas.

I packed up my belongings and relocated to Dallas, Texas to start my own business.

I began leasing oil and gas interest, which included learning title, legal, and working with city government, ordinances, local officials, and property owners. That transitioned naturally to real estate and land acquisition.

As I did more and more oil and gas deals, the owners began contacting me to ask if I was interested in acquiring or purchasing their land.

Do you have an industry specialty or niche?

My specialty is creating an authentic user experience.

I have had the opportunity to go into various neighborhoods and cities and be involved in the entire transformation from start to finish with my development projects.

That includes: Organizing property owners, working with city government, city staff, learning ordinances, rules, and regulations; advocating; and investing in those neighborhoods. It can mean new construction, rehabilitating and repurposing vacant buildings, so they generate economic development, and promoting further development.

There is reason my company name is called "Wildcat." Someone had to be first.

I do it all!

Here is an example of how this played out once in real life: Dallas has one of the longest-running farmers' markets, but the city was looking to close it down. At the time, it was city-owned and operated. I organized the group of business and property owners to lobby at the local and state level to privatize the market and create a new district around the farmers' markets.

I took the oldest commercial building in downtown Dallas, the Liberty Bank Building, which was slated for demolition, bought it for a dollar, and moved it, brick by brick, to a new location a mile away, just adjacent to the historic Dallas Farmers' Market.

The building subsequently became the home of a yoga studio and a well-known downtown bar called the Green Door Public House. Almost immediately, people started walking the streets and sidewalks, and visiting the area which was formerly considered depressed and distressed.

Today, this is the largest residential district in our urban downtown core, with over 4,500 residents in this small area. That was a great success story.

I am also involved with another historic neighborhood in Dallas called the Dallas West End, on the western side of the Central Business District. I reorganized both the neighborhood and business organizations, served as the board's chairman, and rehabbed and renovated one of the neighborhood's last remaining historic buildings — the Purse Building. This building is six stories high and occupies 65,000 square feet. I am also the first woman to own that building and the first person in over 30 years to go in and do any work on it.

What advice do you have for someone entering the commercial real estate industry?

Things always look easier than they are in CRE. Real estate people love to talk about their good deals and their success stories. Nobody ever wants to talk about a bad deal.

But deals are far more challenging than they look. And they take longer.

Some development projects I am involved in take two or three years. Sometimes, they take five to seven years.

You have to work really, *really* hard in those years, put in the hours, and roll up your sleeves.

Sometimes, people think that entrepreneurs have all this free time and flexibility. The reality is that entrepreneurs have to lead the charge to make these businesses successful. They work their asses off and make a lot of sacrifices.

The successful people I know in real estate have done two things:

➢ Worked *hard*

➢ And built relationships

When you get into CRE, the first thing you should do is start cultivating relationships. And a relationship is not always about what you can get out of it, but what you're giving as well. It has got to be reciprocal. If you are offered a seat at the table, take it. Cultivate that connection.

I gave my time when it was needed. I showed up for things. I was visible. I did whatever I needed to get exposure and make those connections.

You have to water the seeds to grow. For a new person starting in this business, you must go the extra mile, show up, be visible, and be present. When I started, I told people they could always count on me. They could call me on weekends or late at night. If they needed extra help or assistance, I would do it.

That gave me a lot of exposure. If there was a meeting with top clients, I got invited as a reward for all my hard work. If we were meeting with a top designer or executive, I got invited. Sitting in those meetings taught me to negotiate and structure deals.

Relationships are probably the most important thing that I nurtured. And nothing beats face-to-face.

Did/do you have a mentor and how did you find him or her?

My biggest mentor was my father. He is also an entrepreneur. He grew up on a farm on the river bottoms of Minnesota, got a factory job, and put himself through technical school. Later, he owned one of southeastern Minnesota's largest boat and car dealerships.

I come from a racing family. You could not tell I was a girl when my dad put me on a sled with my snowmobile suit. The boys and girls all looked the same. At a young age, I was taught to jump in, go after what I wanted, and be part of the conversation.

When I was 19 or 20, I interned at Neiman Marcus. I had an executive manager there who acted almost precisely like Miranda Priestly in *The Devil Wears Prada*. When she hit me with a question, she expected me to know my stuff. She would call me in and hammer me with questions. That really taught me how to perform on the spot.

It also taught me to always research my subject matter — my audience, the person I am pitching to, or anything else I am involved in.

Many of my real estate and construction mentors ended up being men because I work in such a male-dominated industry. I have a bit of a reputation for my No BS attitude, confidence, and even being a little aggressive. I believe that is because of these mentors' influences.

No one gives it a second thought when a man acts that way. But when a woman does, it is taken a little differently.

My mentors taught me to speak up, go for it, and not be a wallflower. If I saw something and felt strongly about it, I should go after it. I was taught not to be run over by the other people — the other *men* — but rather to get in there and fight for what I believed in.

What is the best advice you have received?

I was taught to walk to the beat of my drum at a very young age. My parents told me it's okay to be different, to never let others set my bar or my expectation of myself.

My father has a favorite saying: It is okay to swim with the sharks, so long as you know they can eat you.

This is a cutthroat business. You have to keep that in mind when you are making deals. But if you stay focused on your goal, drown out their noise, and set your own bar, you can accomplish anything you set your mind to.

This is especially important for women and new people just starting out in real estate or business.

What are three skills you need to be in the industry?

My top three skills to succeed in this industry are:

➢ Show up. Ninety percent is just *showing up*

➢ Follow up

➢ Roll up your sleeves and work hard

Showing up

I often say that 90% is *showing up*. You do not need to be the most intelligent person in the room or even the most talented. But you need to be visible, present, and reliable.

I look at all these resumés of all these people who have gone to these important colleges — but talent or smarts is only as good as the person's work ethic.

Hard work always beats talent when talent does not work hard. I do not care where someone went to school. It does not mean diddly if that person does not work hard. I would rather have a kid who is just trying to hustle and arrives at 7:30am ready to work, over the college grad who arrives at 10:30am and thinks he's owed the world. I can teach the hustle kid the other stuff.

Hustle is better than any education.

Following up

This seems like such a no-brainer, right? It is shocking how few people follow up in real estate. Do you know how many deals I have done from calling people back over the years?

When following up, it is essential to know when to talk and when to listen. I am really good at asking questions. By asking questions, I've been able to spot that they might be a better fit for another location, or learn of other potential properties for lease or sale. And I would close the deal that way because I understood better of what they wanted.

Also, phone calls are better than email or texting for following up. Just like visibility is important, so are phone calls.

In-person matters. I have never closed a big deal on a video call or a phone call. I close all big deals in person. I will hop on a plane at five in the morning or be there at midnight if I have to. Nothing is better at closing deals than being visible and present.

Working hard

You probably would not believe me if I told you how many times, I have picked up trash, picked up a paintbrush, climbed a frickin ladder, climbed a fence — you name it, I have probably done it. I have never asked anyone to do something for me that I have not done myself. You need to roll up your sleeves and get dirty. When I am working a deal, I am available 24/7. When you are the owner, or driving the deal, the buck stops with you.

What failure stands out for you and what did you learn?

Fortunately, I am fairly risk tolerant. Working in oil and gas, venture capital, and real estate taught me to adapt to the environment.

But I did have to learn that sometimes things do not work, and you should not take it too personal.

Sometimes, you have a beautiful product in the best location, but it does not click. Consumer perception and tolerance might have something to do with it. But sometimes the vision or space just does not translate. Sometimes, things just do not click, and you need to cut your losses — refocus valuable time elsewhere and exit.

Time is our most valuable resource. When you put your time into an investment, which is not performing for whatever reason, you need to place your time into something else that is.

What are the steps you have taken to succeed in commercial real estate?

Firstly, I take the time to become an expert in whatever I am selling. If I am building in a particular city, I become obsessed with that city or neighborhood. I entrench myself in it, read everything I can, research everything I can, and become the subject matter expert.

I only ever invest in areas that I am personally knowledgeable of. I only invest in markets that I know. If I want to acquire property, I will spend time at the location, boots on the ground, and getting to know the city, business owners, and consumers.

I am successful because I show up and I am visible. I follow up. And I work hard. But I also do one other thing:

You have got to be your own cheerleader. As women, we tend to downplay some of our strengths. We do not like to brag or talk too much about our successes. Men do not seem to suffer from this! They tend not to be too afraid to brag about the great things they have done.

But women do not do it enough. Maybe they do not want to rock the boat because there are so few of us.

You need to cheerlead for yourself. It is also essential to cheerlead for other women, speak up, talk about your successes, and promote yourself.

In this business, you are only ever as good as your last deal. You can score the next big deal, win an award, or be on the cover of the paper. And the next day, it is somebody else.

So really embrace your successes, own them, talk about them, promote them, and use them to push yourself forward.

What question are you asked the most?

"Does she always have this much energy? Are you always this upbeat?"

I have two speeds: Stop and go. And I go pretty darn hard. I am an eternal optimist and super self-motivated.

I can have the most challenging day and get beat up pretty hard — it tends to come all at once — but I believe each day is a new one. Monday is a new week. A new month is a fresh month. And every morning is a reset.

New Day. Start fresh.

So, yes, I really do have this much energy.

What are the greatest challenges you have faced in the industry?

Being a female in a male-dominated industry can be tricky. And sometimes, the women in the industry are not so nice to each other, either.

Women have to work much harder because we are held to different expectations. I have embraced that. Those things that make me different also make me stand out.

Because I have been trained and mentored by many men, my negotiating style sways into the aggressive side. But I have opened a lot of doors because of that.

When you are different, you tend to hear criticisms of your success. That can be tough. But I must push that out and keep swimming, despite the sharks in the water. I got to where I am because I am good at what I do. I work hard. I am not afraid to get my hands dirty. I show up. And I am dependable.

I hope my success paves the way for other women who might be behind me. I firmly believe that it does.

What is the best negotiation tip you have learned?

"Deals that move slow, blow!" In other words: Urgency matters, and if deals linger too long without a response, they tend to go south.

I love the *art* of a deal. It is like a dance. Or a chess game.

Deals always bring surprises. They change constantly. And they can be as frustrating as they are exciting.

You must understand the balance between listening, and asking questions that help you assess the angle or pitch. You need to know when to come on strong and when to back off.

But if a deal moves too slow, it blows! So, you need to know when to make the offer, do the pitch, and do the close.

And when it is time to close, even if it is 10:00pm on a Sunday night, you name the place, and I will be there.

What time management tools or skills do you use?

I am wired as an entrepreneur. I love what I do, and I love my own business. But managing time does present unique challenges. Sometimes, it is difficult for me to find balance.

Time is our most valuable resource. And the more projects you have, the more challenging it becomes to find that balance.

Taking care of my body helps me keep my mind strong. I believe what you do on the inside affects your state of mind. To perform at a high level, you must keep your mind and body strong.

As I have achieved more success, finding that work-life balance has become more complex. But it helps to surround myself with positive people because, if time is so valuable, I prefer to spend it with people who lift me up.

What advice would you give to the next generation of female leaders?

The pandemic was not kind to many of the female real estate executives and business owners I know. Some did not return to the industry and chose a different path in life.

That has created a gap for the newer generation to fill.

About five or six years ago, I decided that I do not need to be someone's best friend to support them. But we can still be encouraging to one another. And I decided to make a conscious effort to cheerlead other female entrepreneurs, writing notes of encouragement and going out of my way to motivate their success and inspire others in the industry.

My other advice for new female leaders is: When you are starting out, many people want to help you. They really want to see you succeed. Take advantage of that.

What organizations or groups do you recommend becoming part of your network?

I recommend getting involved in your community, the city, and organizations that might not be directly in your industry. These can all provide a lot of networking opportunities.

I have served on several City Commissions, boards, and advisory committees. I have been involved with public safety, homelessness, quality of life, economic development, mobility, and urban planning.

Local government has an enormous impact on commercial real estate. I am a big advocate of getting involved in how your city works.

Oh, and remember to vote! Local elections and government have the single biggest impact on our quality of life and daily business.

Looking back, what is one thing you wish you knew at the beginning of your career?

At the start of my career, I was too concerned with being accepted and respected. I paid too much attention to what people thought of me. I felt I had to do bigger and better deals to prove myself.

I know now that you have to be confident in your own success. You have to be comfortable with who you are.

There will always be a bigger and better deal. Do not get caught up in that. Stay focused and set your own standard.

The other thing I would advise is to be more mindful of *time*. Recognize that time is a commodity that cannot be recovered. Looking back, I would probably pass on a few deals that took away time that could have been expended elsewhere. Those deals hooked me because I was too emotionally involved, or I was involved in the community, or I wanted to make an impact, or I felt they would make some statement.

But they just took too much time.

I have learned that the return on your time investment is essential. Sometimes, you just need to let go.

BIO - TANYA RAGAN

Email : info@wildcatmanagement.net

LinkedIn -Tanya Ragan - https://www.linkedin.com/in/tanyaragan/

Instagram -@TanyaARagan - https://www.instagram.com/tanyaaragan/

Twitter -@TanyaARagan - https://twitter.com/TanyaARagan

Facebook -@TanyaARagan - https://www.facebook.com/tanyaaragan/

You Tube -@tanyaragan4485 - https://www.youtube.com/channel/UCe7SGboRcEqmNIg3WnRDUMA

Tanya Ragan, President Wildcat Management Wildcat Management is a woman- owned and operated real estate investment and development company. Wildcat Management takes on mission-driven projects and strategic public-private sector partnerships in the hopes of sparking economic turnaround and community growth. Though Wildcat Management regularly grabs headlines for their cutting- edge work in historic rehabilitation, they have an equally booming business in real estate investing, oil and gas, and venture capital. With a nationwide network of satellite offices and industry relationships, Wildcat also possesses the infrastructure and agility to manage projects and investments across the country Tanya Ragan, founder, and President of Wildcat Management, is an entrepreneur, activist, and leader of the movement to redevelop Downtown Dallas. As a female business-owner and self-made entrepreneur, Tanya is leading the charge for Women in commercial real estate, construction and venture capital.

Tanya was ranked as a top commercial real estate developer in the Dallas Business Journal's annual Book of Lists (2019, 2020, 2021, 2022). Ms. Ragan prides herself in being a subject matter expert and has been recognized by various media news publications, including: • Dallas Business Journal – Top North Texas Top Women owned Business • Dallas Business Journal – Top North Texas Commercial Real Estate Developer • Preservation Dallas - Preservation

Achievement Award for Purse Building Project • City of Dallas - Outstanding Award in Business • Regional Hispanic Contractors Association – Outstanding Executive of the Year • Dallas Business Journal – Most Inspiring Leader • Globe St. – Commercial Real Estate Diversity Champion • Globe St – Women of Influence Award • D CEO - Corporate Leadership Excellence Award • Dallas Business Journal - Best Real Estate Deal Honoree for Purse Building Project • The Business Journals – Top 100 Commercial Real Estate Influencer in U.S. • City of Dallas – Impact Award • Dallas Business Journal - Best Real Estate Deal Honoree for Liberty State Bank Building • Buildings Magazine – Cover Story – The Grand Dame of Dallas • Preservation Dallas – Preservation Achievement Award for Liberty State Bank Building

VALERIE RICHARDSON

Company: ICSC

Years in Commercial Real Estate: 40

How did you get started in commercial real estate and what age?

I was 23 when I started as a Retail Property Manager's Assistant at the Dallas office of the Trammell Crow Company, the largest developer in the country. At the time, I had no concept of the significance of entering the world of commercial real estate development in the early 80's in Texas.

An entry-level position in shopping center management was not particularly glamorous and, to this day, I have enormous respect for those dedicated to the repair of incessant roof leaks, the fending off of the attack of the 7-year cricket invasion, manning the bucket brigade when unseasonably cold weather causes multiple pipes to break, the clean-up after the seasonal return of millions of the dreaded black crow... all for the privilege of chasing down 'fly-by-night' tenants to collect their monthly rent payment. It wasn't long before I recognized that what intrigued me about the real estate business was on the *transaction* side. I believed, with my gender-influenced, inherent knowledge of shopping that I had something valuable to contribute to the team.

Having received my undergraduate degree in Special Education, I was not academically prepared for the finance and document-heavy world of commercial real estate, so I began pursuit of my MBA at night to prepare myself to be a "deal-maker." The only problem was getting accepted into the leasing program. All the leasing agents, specifically from Ivy League MBA programs, were recruited to learn the many aspects of the leasing and development business so they could become a Partner some day – a Partner who would help grow the company by moving to an untapped city and launching a development branch to meet the growth needs of a new community. That's exactly what I wanted to do.

In my view, just because my MBA was from an area university that would have three name changes in 15 years should not matter. I did the work, I had an HP12c Financial Calculator, and I knew what amortization meant, I was good to go! After completing my MBA, I trotted my enthusiastic self over to the recruiting department and told the Recruiting Director that I wanted to be a retail leasing agent. She (note gender reference} laughed congenially and told me that I did not have the correct "pedigree" to lease space, so she suggested I go back to my desk and "file something". Unfortunately, this was not the only time in my career that a *woman* was more of an obstacle than an advocate, but it was the first and certainly the most devastating.

Fortunately, my spirit was unbowed. Believing that "you succeed only because others want you to"[1] set my career on a path that helped circumvent the inevitable obstacles. I was fortunate to have support and valuable guidance from my colleagues. They helped me understand lease documents, assisted with selling skills, and lobbied on my behalf with upper management. I started dressing the part...navy blue suits with the fashion of the day - little rosette neck ties - while still working hard collecting rent and bailing water.

One day, I got the call...first moving into the leasing ranks, then, over the years, seeking out and negotiating with major tenants, implementing new retail developments and eventually being named the second woman partner in the firm.

Do you have an industry specialty or niche?

I have always worked in the retail real estate segment of commercial real estate. My first ten years with the Trammell Crow Company, in the retail division, leasing, managing and building shopping centers in Dallas, Texas established the foundation for career opportunities to come. In 1991, I joined the Barnes & Noble Superstores real estate team, implementing the store growth strategy for the innovative new concept. At that time, bookstores were typically mall-based, small square footage retail shops. There was a movement to create large format stores which presented a comprehensive offering of books in a community-friendly environment. It was truly a 'novel' concept presenting a depth and breadth of reading materials that had never been assembled under one roof. Our team moved quickly and decisively to bring the concept to markets nationwide. We learned how to evaluate market potential and create brand awareness. We grew in our negotiating capabilities as the stores grew from 12,000 to 18,000 to 25,000 square feet over the first year of expansion.

The look and presentation of the stores evolved to include a Starbucks Café, bringing two emerging blockbuster brands together under one roof to create a social gathering place for local communities. Soon after, music and software departments were added to the collection. Imagine trying to lease space in a shopping center while your own requirements keep changing. "You can't copy a moving target!"[2] became our mantra.

I learned how critical it is for a retailer in a highly competitive segment to continually evolve to exceed the customers' expectations. You must stay close to your customer while continually looking for growth opportunities. We opened more than 300 book superstores in the first four years generating over $1 billion in sales - creating value for customers, communities and the company. In retail, the creative component is vital to success. To envision a retail concept that resonates with the public is a thrilling proposition; to "dream more than others think practical. Expect more than others think possible"[3] is what makes great retailers undeniably so.

The experience taught me to be aggressive in deal-making, to take advantage of the excitement created with the expansion of a fresh new concept and to be relentless in that pursuit.

Then there was an opportunity to join the 'softer side.' In 1995, I joined the team at Ann Taylor, Inc. - a national specialty women's apparel chain. It was the first time I had the occasion to work for a woman, a talented merchant with a clear vision for the brand. But iconic brands and leaders can share a similar fate; they rise and fall based on exceeding customer's expectations. A couple of consecutive seasons selecting the wrong color green for your apparel offerings, can make your brand a "peacock one day, a feather duster the next."[4] Particularly in the fashion business, close contact to the brand relationship with the customer is critical. Without a strong understanding of the expectations and preferences of the target customer, product collections can easily stray off track, invoking a brutal response - my boss and mentor was gone. But she left behind a new vision, a budding concept that revitalized the brand by reaching a totally new customer base. I was fortunate to facilitate the creative process with a talented group of merchants, designers, marketing and store design professionals to define and create a new concept – Ann Taylor Loft - that eventually surpassed the legacy brand and brought the company back to prosperity. The lesson, particularly in specialty retail is to "stay nervous and stay humble"[5] - never lose sight of the needs of your customer; constantly invent and reinvent the brand offering to best resonate with their needs and desires.

After 20 years in retail real estate, I reinvented my personal brand offering once again. Joining one of Fortune Magazine's *Best 100 Companies to Work for* – The Container Store - was a career highlight. A much smaller company than I had been involved with previously, the entrepreneurial spirit was very much alive. As with my other retail experiences, growth - smart, profitable, reliable growth - was vital to the very livelihood of the company; but more importantly, at this company, how the process was implemented was even more essential. Collaboration at the highest level created opportunity for exceptional growth and brand performance.

In many retail companies, real estate departments can be isolated from the day-to-day retail operations. They are the 'lone wolves' of the company, disappearing at a moment's notice and returning with a fresh prospect. In a retail company, real estate is a side-line focus, not part of the customer interaction, operating business or current marketing campaign. However, in the right culture, retail real estate professionals have the opportunity to be a part of something bigger... the brands we represent, the relationships we create, the employees and communities we impact...when integrated into the company's DNA ...corporate real estate can generate immensely strategic, productive, profitable and gratifying company growth. It is the collective consciousness that builds a better business. It's recognizing your 'wake' - "how everything you do, and everything you don't do, impacts your business, the people around you, and the world around you, far, far, far more than you can imagine."[6] Those dedicated to retail real estate can contribute incredible value to a retail organization, its brand, employees, customers, vendors, communities and investors...all the shared stakeholders benefit when a company delivers sustained, profitable growth.

After 20 years at The Container Store, the final chapter of my retail real estate career involves a 'mission of the heart' – serving the collective membership through ICSC, the professional trade organization dedicated to the advancement, support and advocacy of our industry.

Our industry, the marketplaces and spaces where people shop, dine, work, play and gather, provides the foundation for thriving communities and economies. Using the experiences of my career, it is a privilege to serve the industry that has shaped my professional and personal life.

What advice do you have for someone entering the commercial real estate industry?

It is important to align your talents and your interests with your desired role. There are many segments and services available in the commercial real estate industry. In addition to the various segments – retail, industrial, office, multi-family, medical – there are different roles – client services, leasing, asset or property management, financial analysis, investments. There is not a right or wrong, a better or worse, it's about what resonates for you. Steve Jobs, the founder of Apple said "…the only way to do great work is to love what you do." Recognizing your personal skills, talents and passion will help you find the best career path.

Did/do you have a mentor and how did you find him or her?

I have been fortunate to have many mentors, both in and out of the industry. Most people are happy (and honored) to share their perspectives and experiences with a colleague or rising professional. There are people you meet who you 'know' you can learn something from, whether it is because of their role or their life experience.

The relationship can start with asking a potential mentor for coffee or lunch and by indicating that you would like to get their feedback on a particular topic. Sometimes it's only one meeting, other times it blossoms into years of friendship. Make the ask, take what you can get and cherish the opportunity.

What is the best advice you have received?

"Believe in yourself." When you believe in yourself, you have confidence in your own talents and abilities. Your own self-confidence influences your productivity and allows you to overcome challenges. People around you can sense when you are confident in your knowledge, your capabilities and your contributions. Believing that you have the potential to make a difference has a positive impact on your life and those around you. Recognizing opportunities, being willing to take calculated risks and pushing yourself to achieve your dreams are all rooted in having faith in yourself.

What are three skills you need to be in the industry?

Do your homework – there is no substitute for market knowledge; it separates those who know what they are talking about from those who are faking it.

Commit to being a lifetime learner – learn about aspects of the industry both inside and outside your specialty. Recognize that the market is constantly changing; stay current and informed. Look for opportunities to sharpen your skills and advance your knowledge, be it financial, negotiating, public speaking, or professional writing. Always invest in developing a 360° view of the industry.

Be someone other people want to work with – the commercial real estate industry is very competitive; brokers and leasing agents are competing for clients, tenants are competing for locations, investors are competing for new ventures. It's important to remember that it is an industry, particularly the retail segment, built on relationships and repeat business. A competitor today could be a client tomorrow. Be respectful, responsive, and reliable.

What failure stands out for you and what did you learn?

It was my first 'deal' or, actually, 'non-deal.' I was a young leasing agent, working to lease a space in a small retail center. I had identified a viable tenant who had interest in the center for their new business. We agreed to deal terms and entered into lease negotiations. I was very anxious to complete the transaction and didn't recognize that I was putting too much pressure on the inexperienced tenant to commit to the deal. Basically, I scared them away.

Through this and many other negotiating experiences, I learned to be much more aware of the other party's perspective.... when to be patient, when to increase the pace, when to provide information and when to pull back. Understanding where the other party "is" in the transaction process is the key to successfully completing the deal, even if it means not completing it.

What are the steps you have taken to succeed in commercial real estate?

Listen-learn-attempt-fail/succeed repeat.

Get comfortable outside your 'comfort zone.' It takes time to become an expert in your chosen area. Relationship building, transaction assessment, and negotiating skills don't come naturally to most people. You have to listen and learn from others, make attempts, be willing to 'fail forward' – use mistakes as a step toward success, and then do it again tomorrow. The lesson, particularly in retail real estate, is to "stay alert, stay nimble and stay humble".[5] Never lose sight of the requirements of your customer; constantly invent and reinvent your offering to best resonate with their needs.

What question are you asked the most?

Who took your job at [*old company*]? Members of our industry can lift you and humble you, sometimes on the same occasion. I have been fortunate to represent exceptional retail brands over my career. My life has been enriched by the relationships and the opportunities I have had. But it is always important to remember that your professional (not personal) value can be closely related to the brand you represent.

In a transaction business, the ability to facilitate deals is paramount. Knowing the "right" people is the key to developing a successful business. It only stands to reason that when you depart from an opportunity-creating role, savvy professionals want to know who is next in line.

It is not personal, but it is critical to remember that one you leave one role for another, your reputation and your character are what follow you.

What are the greatest challenges you have faced in the industry?

For me, regardless of the comment in Question 1, it was not "other women" or "being a woman in a man's business." The challenges have been less about gender and more about economics - learning to navigate the peaks and valleys that naturally occur in the real estate industry. While I have had many fortunate opportunities in my career journey, I found that the momentum in my career was occasionally interrupted by events much more impactful that losing a deal.

At the end of 1986, Congress passed a law that changed the way real estate partnerships were accounted for; the tax benefits associated with partnerships went away, virtually overnight and nobody saw it coming. It took some time, but eventually it dismembered the way my company had structured its business. My take-away from this experience was that you always have to be a legislative advocate for your business, both in your local market and on the national level.

Each decade has experienced some sort of economic upheaval - the 70's energy crisis, inflation, the 80's savings and loan crisis, the 90's dot-com bubble collapse and the 2008 subprime mortgage crisis triggering the Great Recession all had significant impacts on the real estate industry.

In a transaction business, you are subject to the ebb and flow of the market. Be willing to re-evaluate your business strategy, make adjustments as needed, and work to capitalize on opportunities presented by the current conditions.

What is the best negotiation tip you have learned?

Listen more than you talk. There is a tendency to try to 'convince' the other party of your position rather than to better understand the other party's interests. Active listening helps you identify areas of agreement and find possible resolutions. Use your body language (leaning in) and brief replies to demonstrate you are paying attention. Summarize what you heard the other person say to make sure you are clear on their position. Use open-ended questions – "can you help me understand" instead of "why."

Use 'silence as a tactic' to increase pressure on the other party to talk, possibly revealing information that could benefit your position. It allows you to keep control of the conversation while making the other party outline their concerns or requirements.

Regardless of your negotiation style, the goal in any negotiation should be to create the opportunity for a 'win-win' outcome. Any negotiation ending with unbalanced terms sets the stage for a strained business relationship. In an industry where repeat business and long-term relationships establish the greatest success, 'Win-Win' always wins.

What time management tools or skills do you use?

I have learned to be deliberate in allocating my time and maximizing my efficiency so that I can be productive in all areas of my life. Personal well-being is critical to your ability to consistently meet your obligations in both your personal and professional life. Prioritizing your health, sleep, exercise and personal time is a necessity not a luxury.

I highly recommend referring to some classic time management business books to assist you in developing a routine that works best for you. Try the 1997 best-seller, *'Don't Sweat the Small Stuff...and It's All Small Stuff"*. Dr. Richard Carlson outlines how practicing patience, compassion and gratefulness helps us manage our priorities and improves how other people feel about us. David Allen's *"Getting Things Done"*, published in 2001, shares tips for increasing productivity, staying focused, and transforming the way you work.

In a busy business and personal life, managing priorities can certainly be challenging. Consider using technology to your advantage – some recommendations to consider are Microsoft Planner, Smartsheet, Asana, Full Life Planner or Monday.com to allow you to prioritize, plan your activities and implement effectively.

Above all, take care of yourself first, then the rest becomes manageable.

What advice would you give to the next generation of female leaders?

The advice I received when starting my career is still relevant today. "Believe in yourself." Give yourself the best opportunity to succeed and contribute value by investing in your own career – through education, experience and building strong relationships, and in your own well-being – prioritizing all aspects of good health, and self-care. Be sure to take advantage of any training and career development opportunities and to create a support network of healthy relationships and mentors. Recognize that setbacks and challenges happen; use them as growth and learning opportunities. Developing self-confidence, meaningful relationships and personal resilience are the foundations of a successful career (and life).

It encourages you to make thoughtful decisions, take calculated risks and overcome unanticipated obstacles. By having faith in yourself and your abilities, learning to prioritize effectively and embracing both opportunities and challenges, you can create the professional and personal life you envision.

What organizations or groups do you recommend becoming part of your network?

The best way to build your network is to consider both professional and personal opportunities to interact with others that share your career and individual interests. National and local chapter professional organizations like ICSC, CREW, ULI, and NAIOP provide industry specific networking, deal-making and education opportunities that enhance your exposure and career development. Building personal networks in charitable organizations, book clubs, and affinity groups broadens your perspective and exposes you to other viewpoints.

Looking back, what is one thing you wish you knew at the beginning of your career?

My commercial real estate career has led me on a journey I could not have imagined when I started. Knowing what I know now, I would have leveraged my relationships and developed a strong network of peers and mentors earlier in my career. Starting out in the business, I was more focused on tasks and accomplishments than people. Over the years I have learned that my greatest professional and personal growth experiences have come from connections that I made both in and outside of the real estate industry. My relationships, partnerships and friendships offered much more richness to my career than any transaction could have. The steps and missteps, the opportunities and challenges, and the many people who have provided me guidance, perspective and friendship along the way have helped me become the person I am today. For their time, interest and unwavering support, I will always be grateful.

*****

[1] Trammell Crow

[2] Len Riggio

[3] Howard Schultz

[4] Sally Frame Kasaks

[5] Gordon Segal

[6] Kip Tindell

BIO - VALERIE RICHARDSON

Valerie Richardson brings expertise from over 40 years in retail estate, working for several national bands. She is currently the Chief Operating Officer of ICSC, the professional trade association of the Marketplaces Industry, a position she has held since February 2021. She oversees day-to-day administrative and operational functions of ICSC collaborating on marketing, membership, volunteer engagement, talent development and ICSC's portfolio of programs and services.

Ms. Richardson previously served as Vice President of Real Estate for The Container Store, Inc. from September 2000 until February 2021. Prior to joining The Container Store, Ms. Richardson was Senior Vice President – Real Estate and Development for Ann Taylor, Inc., the specialty women's apparel retailer, where she administered the company's store expansion strategy for Ann Taylor and Ann Taylor Loft. Before Ann Taylor, Ms. Richardson was Vice President of Real Estate and Development of Barnes & Noble, Inc., the country's largest bookselling retailer. Prior to Barnes & Noble, Ms. Richardson was a Partner in the Shopping Center Division of the Dallas-based developer, Trammell Crow Company.

An active industry participant and advocate, Ms. Richardson was elected Chairman of the ICSC for the 2018-2019 term, after having served on that 45,000+ Marketplaces industry trade organization's Board of Trustees since 2004. She served as ICSC's first Chairman from an active retailer and the fifth female Chair in the organization's history.

Since 2018, Ms. Richardson has served on the Board of Directors for Kimco Realty Corp., North America's largest publicly traded owner and operator of open-air, grocery-anchored shopping centers. In 2023, she joined the Board of Directors of American Healthcare REIT, a large healthcare-focused real estate investment trust, with a diverse portfolio of medical office buildings, senior housing communities, skilled nursing facilities and integrated senior living campuses.

Ms. Richardson served as a Trustee at Baylor Scott & White Medical Center – Plano from 2010 – 2016 where she chaired the Medical Center's Quality Committee. Ms. Richardson earned an

M.B.A. in Real Estate from the University of North Texas and a B.S. in Education from Texas State University. She resides in Dallas, Texas; is married, has two children and one amazing grandchild.

ALICE SEALE

Company: Seale Realty Advisors

Years in Commercial Real Estate: 30

How did you get started in commercial real estate and what age?

My retail real estate business began when I moved to Dallas after graduating from The University of Mississippi due to accomplished women such as Mary Kay, Ebby Holiday, and Mary Crowley already residing there.

National companies had to employ a specified number of women. Because of this, a worldwide copier company hired me. After finishing a three-month sales training program, my territory in Dallas consisted of newly constructed office buildings along the LBJ corridor that would benefit from our copier technology. It included cold calling, presentations, copier demonstrations, entertaining clients, time management, and sale closure.

The Copier Company's regional offices were in Dallas, home to a group of salespeople, customer service agents, service representatives, and management. I earned $30,000 a year and received a company car and benefits.

I over-achieved my goals during my first two years as a sales representative. During a national convention, my regional manager recommended me to the Vice President of Sales as a candidate for the sales manager position. We met for the first time in a hotel meeting room. When he inquired if I was interested in the sales manager position, I was ecstatic to discover the opportunity for a promotion. As our talk continued, he asked if I had questions about the sales manager position and its duties to the company. I responded, "I'm concerned about the money offered." My Dallas friends earned $30,000 monthly from commercial real estate and the oil and gas industry commissions, whereas my annual salary was only $30,000. When he avoided discussing money, I realized it was not for me.

I was eager to begin a career in commercial real estate. After fulfilling my real estate license requirements, I interviewed for prospective commercial real estate companies.

The Hank Dickerson Company is where I began my career in commercial real estate; he believed that retail leasing presented an opportunity for women. The company offered an excellent real estate sales training curriculum and mentorship.

In my second year of real estate, the recession was the best thing to have happened in building work habits, tenaciousness, and grit. No way was I going to return to my small hometown in Southeast Missouri, so I had to make a commission job work for me. I also believed that your next phone call could alter the course of my life, and I adhere to this even today.

My family and friends questioned why I would not accept a conventional career. And my response was that I desired to climb the mountain peaks no one else would climb due to their terrain and altitude. I am still climbing and challenged by the terrain and altitude, yet I believe in myself.

In my real estate career, I had the opportunity to work for retailers and developers. When a friend in real estate informed me, she had been hired as the head of real estate for a large restaurant chain to grow their nationwide rollout of sites, I landed my first job in retail site selection. This opportunity led me to other national site selection opportunities, such as; Tuesday Morning, Blockbuster, and Fantastic Sam's. Al's Formal Wear, Zale Corp, and Card & Party Outlet to visit and conduct business in every large and regional U.S. city. Other retailers and developers have benefited from my knowledge of real estate markets.

Working with developers allows you to impact projects that alter the lives of others and increase the value of the project for the owner. I worked for a real estate development company in Manchester, Connecticut. The developer had purchased 100 acres of land along the Rio Grande border in Edinburg, Texas, to construct a 1.3 million square feet open-air shopping mall.

I contacted any retailer who would benefit the market and its growth; what fun for me. The Rio Grande has a place in my heart to deliver a project that would increase the sales revenue for the county, and the retail employees would have corporate benefits.

In addition, the company's chief executive officer permitted me to implement a long-held ambition to host a networking luncheon where women in commercial real estate could meet retail company decision-makers. The name of the luncheon was the SMART TALK SMART WOMEN Luncheon. For over a decade, a luxury hotel hosted luncheons in December where women in retail and commercial real estate could network with retail tenants attending the venue, panelists, and job seekers. According to rumors about women attending luncheons, we can discuss the weather, work, and family in an hour and be on our way.

List of the Retail Panelists:

➤ American Girl

➤ Barnes & Noble

➤ Crayola Experience

➤ Estee Lauder

➤ Favor The Kind

➤ Foot Locker

➤ JC Penney

➤ Limited Brands

➤ Macy's

➤ Neiman

➤ Peacock Alley

➤ Starwood Hotels

➤ Tiffany & CO

Also, I worked for a pension fund Clarion Partners, out of their Dallas office. My responsibility was to lease a high-end shopping

Center in Waterside Shoppes, Naples, Florida. Traveling all over the U.S. was a dream to review high-end shopping centers and work with high-end tenants. The management in the Dallas office was the best I ever had, and I also made life longs friends.

Then I have been a solo practitioner for the last ten years, and all my networking, relationships, and market knowledge have paid off. I am working with incredible tenants in their expansion of their as consultants for retailers, developers, and investment sales. The solo practitioner allows me to be involved in different projects.

Do you have an industry specialty or niche?

I began my career in retail, and that has been my primary emphasis. I have worked with retailers on the growth of their stores in major and regional US markets. And leased developments on the landlord's side. Over the past few years, I have also had the opportunity to engage in investment sales.

What advice do you have for someone entering the commercial real estate industry?

Enter the real estate sector with all your heart, examine the best producers' work patterns, establish a network, and join an industry association.

Did/do you have a mentor and how did you find him or her?

Find your industry tribe as a priority; I have had a company tribe for 20 years. This group of women in commercial real estate gives you an opportunity for a source, and they have your back. No one understands everything, and as the real estate industry evolves, we all have questions and want further knowledge.

I am a member of a group of senior professional women in Dallas called Sounding Board. Each member has a unique business background, including attorneys, marketing directors, certified public accountants, health and nutrition specialists, and life coaches. Hearing their opinion from these women and also another networking opportunity. Additionally, we read and discuss business books.

What is the best advice you have received?

People may not recognize you outside of the context in which you met them.

Never arrive late for a scheduled appointment.

Not all businesses are profitable.

What are the three skills you need to be in the industry?

> The ability to successfully communicate vocally and in writing

> To continue in the profession for any length of time, you must demonstrate honesty to clients and coworkers

> The desire comes from inside

What failure stands out for you and what did you learn?

I have learned the hard way that I must first listen to what a person is saying before asking questions.

This is where my ACT contact data came in handy, allowing me to offer comments and keep track of past talks.

What are the steps you have taken to succeed in commercial real estate?

Participating in the organizations of your industry. Sign up for a committee.

Always identify yourself first; never rely on people to recollect your name. This is one of the best recommendations my mentor has ever given me!

Do not hesitate to pick up the phone, write an email, or request an introduction.

When a call comes in, you should first listen and then deliberate your response.

RETURN EVERY PHONE CALL!

Participate in local charitable organizations that interest you.

Understand the importance of time management.

Develop a morning ritual. My routine includes solitude, coffee, and exercise.

Have a business book that you are currently reading.

What question are you asked the most?

Most frequently, I am asked "How I compiled a list of high-end retail tenants and residential interior design clients."

I was the leasing agent for a high-end shopping complex in Naples, Florida, Clarion Real Estate Partners was the landlord. I had the chance to develop contacts with the real estate departments of the shopping center's present tenants, including MaxMara, Saks, Louis Vuitton, Ralph Lauren, Tiffany & Co., and Neiman Marcus. With my gained knowledge of the shopping center's high-end tenants, I was able to contact all of the other high-end tenants. It was my dream job!!!

As the Director of Leasing for a Dallas-based Design Center ignited my passion for residential showroom design. I got the chance to visit to all the design centers around the United States to learn about manufacturing. In the realm of design, there are both major corporations and individuals that bring their ideas to market.

This is an industry that was once exclusive to interior design professionals; however, its policies have grown increasingly permissive, and several manufactures are now operating showrooms in retail shopping areas.

What are the greatest challenges you have faced in the industry?

Dallas, Texas is a business-friendly city that is home to a large number of real estate developers, national real estate companies, and brokers. The greatest difficulty is keeping up with transactions and new ventures. No one desires to hear outdated market information. To remain competitive, you must attend local and national real estate events and study industry publications. Develop a network of colleagues with whom you may trade information.

You can never make too many cold calls or network enough.

What is the best negotiation tip you have learned?

Place yourself across from them in the meeting room.

Practice deep breathing.

Ensure your lower back is again against the chair's bottom seat.

Listen to hear.

What time management tools or skills do you use?

It has worked for me to prepare my day in advance, so that it is already organized before I begin my workday. In addition, I prioritize my list depending on what will create revenue. Using the ACT database for contact management for the past twenty years has allowed me to have client information on my computer and cell phone.

My calendar is essential for avoiding multiple bookings in Outlook. When I organize a meeting or lunch, I find it convenient to send a calendar acceptance with the time and location. The event will then be added to your calendar.

What advice would you give to the next generation of female leaders?

Dallas, Texas is a business-friendly city with numerous real estate developers, major corporations, and brokers; the number of women in our industry will continue to rise.

Keep up with transactions and new enterprises to remain competitive; no one wants to hear obsolete market knowledge; be the expert.

Create a network of peers with whom you may exchange information and mentor younger women.

Our glass ceiling has been smashed!

What organizations or groups do you recommend becoming part of your network?

I would propose starting with real estate alums from your institution. I would email them, introducing myself and asking about their real estate expertise and if they have any career recommendations.

If there are any graduates in the same city, request 15 minutes in their office to speak with them. Before the meeting, they should research the organization online, read the individual's LinkedIn page, and think of questions to ask. After the meeting, SEND them a message of appreciation for their time. Then, once you have chosen a firm, contact them to inform them of your decision and to express your gratitude for their time.

During your review of their LinkedIn page, consider the organizations they belong to; this may inspire you. Real estate alums of your university may be a good starting point. I would write them an email introducing myself, requesting their real estate knowledge, and, if suitable, providing career advice.

If any grads reside in the same city, schedule a 15-minute meeting at their place of employment. Before the visit, they should conduct internet research on the company, evaluate their LinkedIn profile, and prepare questions. After the meeting, SEND an expression of gratitude. Then, once you have selected a company, contact them to advise them of your decision and to offer your appreciation for their support.

While examining their LinkedIn page, you should evaluate the organizations they are affiliated with since this may inspire you.

Then I would join your city's local and national real estate associations.

Looking back, what is one thing you wish you knew at the beginning of your career?

Continue to educate yourself on the evolving local and national real estate markets and technologies.

BIO - ALICE SEALE

Alice Seale is the principal of Seale Realty Advisors. She has counseled national retailers or developers on their portfolios for the past 11 years by offering recommendations to the executive team and implementing decisions. Also, represented clients in the purchase or sale of real estate for their portfolios.

Prior to joining Seale Realty Advisors, she represented Trammell Crow Company leasing of a 500,000-square-foot project for a residential design center. She leased Waterside Shoppes, a high-end luxury retail shopping center in Naples, Florida. A Connecticut developer opened a Dallas office for a 500,000-square-foot ground up development in Edinburg, Texas. She was responsible for the tenant mix and implementation of the project.

She worked with national and regional retailers in the store expansion and portfolio management for retailers for Tuesday Morning, Blockbuster, Zale's, ICBY, and Fantastic Sam's.

In 2005, Alice inaugurated SMART TALK SMART WOMEN Lunch an annual lunch for women in the retail real estate to increase their exposure to senior-level retail real estate professionals. She believed commercial real estate was a great business for women and provided a venue.

She is also D Magazine CEO Power Broker, active member in International Council of Shopping Center, Deals in Heels. Volunteer and mentor to women in the first five years of commercial real estate career.

Alice Z. Seale

aseale@sealerealtyadvisors.com

214 707 6806 cell

972 387 8002 office

KARLA SMITH

Company: SRS Real Estate Partners

Years in Commercial Real Estate: 19

How did you get started in commercial real estate and what age?

I began my career in commercial real estate in 2003 as a 2nd career. I had a great job with a Fortune 100 company, managed a successful sales team, was recognized as a Top 10 sales manager, and was offered a promotion to lead a division in the summer of 2003. I liked working with my team, but I had a raw passion for real estate. I did not know what I did not know but was always intrigued by retail shopping centers, the experience they offered, why they lacked certain brands, how the developments were put together and had overall interest in the details of branding and emerging concepts. I got an unexpected push of confidence while having an impromptu conversation with a long-time real estate veteran at a social event. Speaking to him gave me a new composure and perspective to pursue a real estate career. His expressed confidence that I would be successful made me think harder about what I wanted to do. It did not make the decision easy but nudged me to follow my passion for real estate and I have never looked back.

Do you have an industry specialty or niche?

I specialize in Retail Tenant Representation in CRE, assisting national retailers with strategic rollouts, new store site selection and disposition in the southern US. My niche started as a grocery specialist working with Sprouts Farmers Market on their first expansion in the US outside of Arizona. My partner and I were their exclusive tenant rep team in north Texas. We strategized, identified, negotiated and executed 25 Sprouts locations over a 15-year period. Developing an acumen with landlords and developers and managing numerous transactions with sizeable anchor tenants, helped direct me to anchor tenant representation and has expanded my client base over the years to include national retailers such as Target, Cabela's, At Home, Macys, Michaels, Lifetime Fitness, Pet Supplies Plus et al.

What advice do you have for someone entering the commercial real estate industry?

I would advise someone getting into the CRE industry to be a self-starter, work whatever hours it takes, and incorporate networking early into your career.

Did/do you have a mentor and how did you find him or her?

When I entered commercial real estate (CRE), I was hired by a brokerage looking for an entry level person to assist one of the lead landlord brokers at the firm. I did not intentionally seek a mentor. I did not know better but on the day, I started I was reassigned to a respected tenant rep broker. I did not understand the importance of mentorship and the impact a good mentor can have on your career. My specific mentorship was somewhat by chance but established a solid foundation for me in the industry. My mentor became my business partner and lifelong friend. His mentorship paved the way for me to establish relationships, learn best practices, navigate the CRE business, and maintain character in an ever-changing industry.

What is the best advice you have received?

The best advice I ever received is to be service driven, not fee driven. This is a unique commission-based industry, so the advice has considerable impact. If you focus on your clients, help them achieve their goals, and work at making their needs a priority, you will build long lasting relationships and proudly be part of your client's success. Fees will work themselves out.

What are three skills you need to be in the industry?

Three skills that have helped me succeed in the CRE industry are communication, persistence and integrity. These three skills work together well and, when used in tandem, provide thorough evaluation of opportunities and foster client growth.

What failure stands out for you and what did you learn?

Failure is good if you learn from it. One of my most memorable failures was when I was entering the business and applied to an iconic brokerage firm. They evaluated my application, along with several personality tests and a face-to-face interview. It was a nerve-racking process as an older 'newbie' now determined to change careers. At the end of the interview they told me I was not cut out to be a broker and that my personality qualities showed I would not succeed in the business. It shattered my confidence and created uncertainty about my path and next steps. But only temporarily. I took a deep breath, wrote off the opinion I could not control, and kept interviewing.

What are the steps you have taken to succeed in commercial real estate?

To succeed in CRE I have worked long hours, persevered through changing cycles, worked to establish my own brand, to be a trustworthy advisor to my colleagues and clients, and strive to always take the high road when things swerve.

What question are you asked the most?

The question I get asked most is how to balance a successful full time brokerage career as a female with family responsibilities and raising children. For me, I work long hours but leverage the flexibility of my schedule to keep family a priority.

What are the greatest challenges you have faced in the industry?

The greatest challenges I have had to face in the industry are adjusting to long deal cycles (sometimes years), adapting to a commission based income that can be inconsistent, understanding a broker's position in a transaction, and accepting that you work on more deals that do not materialize than those that do.

What is the best negotiation tip you have learned?

A tip I would offer on how to negotiate is to think like your clients. In my case, I try to think like a retailer and be an extension of their real estate department. Regardless of the dynamics of a transaction, add value by understanding your clients' needs and requirements and be persistent to achieve them. Know what they need and prioritize these things in a negotiation.

What time management tools or skills do you use?

I manage my time by prioritizing my client's needs. Regardless of the task, I try to respond and provide information for those things that my client's need first for them to be successful at their job.

What advice would you give to the next generation of female leaders?

I would advise the next generation of female leaders to be confident, lean in, and be inclusive. Do not waste energy on what you cannot control and, especially for young women, do not swerve when the business gets swervy.

What organizations or groups do you recommend becoming part of your network?

I recommend brokers get involved in industry specific groups such as ICSC, NTCAR (in north TX), CREW (CRE women) for educational and networking purposes. Also, local interest groups that offer exposure to smaller groups for networking across business categories and markets.

Looking back, what is one thing you wish you knew at the beginning of your career?

One thing I wish I knew at the beginning of my career was that this business is not personal. It can be rough, tensions can get strong, stakes can get high, and it can require thick skin. There are sometimes large transactions and big egos in the room, but I have learned to take my deserved seat at the table and take the high road when others are unable to.

BIO - KARLA SMITH

Karla Smith is a leader in the industry and specializes in big box and national tenant representation throughout the states of Texas, Oklahoma, Louisiana, and Arkansas. She joined SRS in 2020 in the Dallas/Ft. Worth office and joined SRS' Board of Members in 2021.

With 19 years of experience in retail real estate, Karla was a partner at UCR prior to its merger with CBRE in 2015 and has accumulated an impressive list of clients as well as accolades for her work in the industry. Karla currently manages new store site selection for many national and regional accounts such as Target, At Home, Macy's, Michael's, Puttery, Pacific Dental Services, AT&T, Frost Bank, Luna Grill and Maple Street Biscuit Company. She also worked on an extensive 15 year rollout strategy with Sprouts Farmers Market in North Texas, and expansions for Cabela's, Pet Supplies Plus, Lifetime Fitness, Planet Fitness, 5-11 Tactical, Blockbuster, Fuddruckers, Core Power Yoga, and Boot Barn..

Karla is highly regarded in the industry, and her advice is sought after by many professionals. Karla has successfully weathered a myriad of industry and economic challenges, maintains a positive attitude, perseveres, actively recruits, and promotes the industry to the next generation. She a contributor in the book Winning Ways in Commercial Real Estate and is an often-quoted resource for publications such as D CEO and the Dallas Business Journal. Locally, Karla has been selected as one of the Dallas Business Journal's Heavy Hitters three times and was recognized as D CEO's Best Commercial Real Estate Broker five times. Her lease for Target in Preston Center in Dallas, a particularly complex location with unique issues, won the 2018 Best Retail Deal in D Magazine, and she has been regularly recognized in the Top 10 by SRS, at CBRE and UCR during her tenure, and as a Power Broker by Real Estate Forum. She was also nominated to receive the NTCAR Stemmons Award for exemplifying highest standards as a commercial real estate professional.

Karla is a graduate of the University of Texas at Dallas and is involved with many industry organizations. She has served as the Texas Programs Committee Chair for ICSC, and as the Retail Committee

Chair and on the executive board for NTCAR. She is a founding member of Deals in Heels, a local networking group of professional women in retail real estate that educates and encourages the growth of women in the industry as well as the Exec Chair for SOAR, a national community of women producers at SRS. In her free time, she enjoys spending time at the lake with family and friends and giving back to the community through faith-based organizations.

JAN (CYCON) TRUE, CRRP, CRX, CSM

Company: True Retail Solutions, LLC

Years in Commercial Real Estate: 41

How did you get started in commercial real estate and what age?

I was 22 years young when I started in commercial real estate! I was working as a paralegal at my dad's legal practice. The office was across a bridge on Avenue of the Stars in Los Angeles, California. The bridge was connected to the Century City Mall (that was what it was called at the time – 1982) I would go sit on a bench and eat my lunch in the great Southern California sunshine (it was an outdoor mall) and people watch. I started looking around, wondering how a mall operated, who ran things, how does maintenance get handled, security and landscaping get taken care of, etc. I literally found a mall directory, located the mall office, and walked up stairs to their office location and asked for the owner. Back then it was owned by a small group of private investors; one of the owners had his office inside and he was there. After being grilled and stonewalled by the snarky receptionist about not having an appointment etc. a gentleman walked by saying he was going to lunch. I politely asked him if he was the mall owner (I was so naïve – ha!) he said "yes" and I offered to buy him lunch if he could allow me 15 minutes of his valuable time. He was very curious, invited me straight back to his office, and we talked for almost two hours! He asked me how much notice to quit I would have to give my dad (I said two weeks of course) and he hired me on the spot! Doing what? To be the receptionist and he moved Ms. Snarky to a desk behind the lobby wall to do administrative work. I wondered what ever happened to her………

Do you have an industry specialty or niche?

More than 40 years of experience in every aspect of Retail Properties. A seasoned veteran in the Retail, Mixed Use, Property Space. Tightly focused and highly targeted Management Operations,

Leasing, Vendor Procurement, Construction and Tenant Build Out supervision, Management, Development, Acquisitions, Dispositions, City Relations, Budgeting, Lease Administration, Capital Expense Projects, Marketing, Team and Relationship Building, Strategic Planning, and more.

What advice do you have for someone entering the commercial real estate industry?

It is ok to CHANGE YOUR MIND! Give yourself permission to pivot. Whether it is where you start college, what studies you focus on, personal relationships, first jobs (will most probably NOT be your life job), companies you commit to, every aspect of your life. Allow evolution, creation, acceptance, forgiveness, and patience.

Did/do you have a mentor and how did you find him or her?

I have had the fortunate pleasure of having several, Mavis Northern was my supervisor/boss at a smaller retail property firm in Santa Monica, California and was extremely generous with words of wisdom and guidance. Charlie Gill, my supervisor/boss for a large retail property management company; gave me my first opportunity to be the General Manager of a Super Regional Mall in Southern California (more than 1.2 million square feet) always believed in me, supported me, and best audience for my jokes. I would be remiss if I also did not mention that mentors come in many forms, my parents, my friends, city and civic leaders, professional colleagues, and most importantly, God.

What is the best advice you have received?

Oh my, I have received so much great advice, it is hard to narrow it down. I would say from Mavis, "Do not take it personal." Being in the mall and retail property sector of commercial real estate comes with lots of what people consider "negative." Constant complaints, challenges, verbal attacks, etc. You must grow a thick skin quickly and realize your tenants are not going to call you to wish you Happy Birthday, but they will call and demand a rent reduction.

What are three skills you need to be in the industry?

> **Patience** – everything will take longer than you anticipate or want

> **Flexibility** – roll with the punches, create a path, when they zig – you zag, every day is different. Embrace change

> **Ethics** – your reputation is everything. Your words matter. No matter where you navigate or grow in commercial real estate, it is a very small world and people have long memories

What failure stands out for you and what did you learn?

My failure was putting too much trust in a former business partner and allowing them to have a bigger position of "power" and decision-making capability for the company. The lesson learned is when you have the choice of giving up equity or position in a company, make sure YOU are in the seat of control. Control your own destiny.

What are the steps you have taken to succeed in commercial real estate?

I have never really looked at my career as taking steps. My career has never been on a straight path. Some steps I will share as words of wisdom, at least they have served me well.

Always ask questions and never stop. Ask "How does that work?" "Who makes that happen?" "How did that get there?" "Why did someone decide to do it that way?"

I truly believe I have grown in my industry most by learning, and you cannot learn without asking questions, then find the answers and solutions. If you are not solving, creating, moving, inquiring, you will become stagnant and irrelevant, and no one wants to be irrelevant.

I also cannot emphasize how important it is to network with others. It is important to always widen your circle of relationships and connections, do not limit yourself to your industry. I have always said "everyone has something to offer" and I have learned so much by asking and learning from others.

Another step is creating opportunity for yourself. I have been fortunate to have been hired by literally showing up at someone's office and explaining why they need to hire me, actually it happened three different times, once in newspaper advertising sales, once in radio commercial sales, and once finding the owner of a mall in Los Angeles; wondering how a mall worked, finding the mall office and owner and convincing him he needed to hire me. That is how I started my retail property management career in 1982. (See question #1)

What question are you asked the most?

"Where do you get all your positive energy?"

What are the greatest challenges you have faced in the industry?

Being a woman in a man's industry, hands down the greatest challenge. When I was gaining momentum as a General Manager of very large malls; I would attend professional conferences of industry peers and I literally would be one of maybe 10 women in a room of 1,000 men.

It takes time for your male peers and counterparts to take you seriously and believe you bring something to the table so to speak. I truly had to earn respect in order to have a voice. (Those that know me are rolling their eyes right now thinking I am never quiet! Ha!)

Another important and extremely frustrating challenge is my male counterparts being paid up to 40% more than me for doing the same job, and much less successfully.

What is the best negotiation tip you have learned?

There are actually four (4) tips; I am a Paul Harris Fellow of Rotary Clubs International and they have the "The Four-Way Test" – I embrace it for all aspects of my life, personal and professional:

1. Is it the TRUTH?

2. Is it FAIR to all concerned?

3. Will it build GOODWILL and BETTER FRIENDSHIPS?

4. Will it be BENEFICIAL to all concerned?

I think of "better friendships" in business negotiations as "better relationships."

What time management tools or skills do you use?

I manage my time not so well! I know that sounds crazy, but it can be a challenge with today's distractions. I am just being honest! Some days I am completely focused and "slay the day." Some days I get distracted by "noise" around us, social media, news, and flat out "squirrel" moments. (Remember Dug the dog in the movie 'UP?')

What advice would you give to the next generation of female leaders?

Do not take "NO" for an answer, no just means "not now." Females by nature are more compassionate, understanding, smart, understanding, supportive, nurturing just to name a few traits. EMBRACE THEM, be strong in your convictions, ideas, and decision making. ASK FOR IT, no one is going to offer.

What organizations or groups do you recommend becoming part of your network?

➤ ICSC

➤ Rotary Club – your local chapter – service above self

If you have a project, you are working on in a certain city attend Planning and Zoning Meetings, City Council meetings, etc. Learn the process and get to know the folks that could be deciding the destiny of your project.

Looking back, what is one thing you wish you knew at the beginning of your career?

Your starting point to your ending point will not be a straight line! I have such a diverse background, in so many different areas, and NOT all in commercial real estate. All experience is good experience, never think of failures and mistakes as forever.

BIO - JAN (CYCON) TRUE, CRRP, CRX, CSM

Ms. True has over 40 years of extensive retail property experience. Born and raised in Los Angeles, she relocated to Dallas 1999 to manage a super-regional mall of 1.6 million square feet for the mall group Macerich. Jan is tightly focused and highly targeted professional executive consultant.

Jan has the following professional experience:

DLC Management – Regional Manager for 1 million sq. ft. Village at Allen outdoor mall; and two other smaller centers in Dallas. NetCo Investments, Inc. – acquisitions, dispositions, operations, leasing, construction management, marketing, property management and asset management. Beck Ventures – Dallas Midtown Project – member of executive team for mall management, leasing, marketing and redevelopment planning team. Urban Partners at West Village Dallas – Director of Property Management for a three City Block Mixed Used Development in Uptown Dallas. General Growth Partners – now Brookfield – Business Development Manager at two super regional malls for all temporary in-line spaces, carts and kiosks. General Manager for two super regional malls in California for The O'Connor Group and Urban Retail Partners

Entrepreneur and founder for 6 years building an online coupon firm and an online meal ordering service.

Jan has the following professional accreditations and achievements:

ICSC – Certified Retail Real Estate Professional (CRRP); Senior Certified Shopping Center Manager (SCSM); Certified Retail Property Executive (CRX); Redevelopment and Housing Commissioner for the City of Anaheim, California. Member of Deals in Heels. Board Member of Rotary Club (Paul Harris Fellow); DFIMA, YMCA, American Heart Association, Dallas Visitors and Convention Bureau (Visit Dallas)

Top Female Executive Award Nominee North Dallas Corridor 2015

Known as "Nicki Network" because of deep rooted relationships in all aspects of retail properties; vendors, tenants, landlords, developers, brokers, etc.

EMAIL - trueretailsolutions@gmail.com

LinkedIn Profile - https://www.linkedin.com/in/jan-cycon-true-crrp-crx-csm-2a1179/

Lynn Van Amburgh

Company: Weitzman

Years in Commercial Real Estate: 42

How did you get started in commercial real estate and what age?

I was 24 and working at what was First National Bank in Dallas in the Real Estate group. I kept seeing deals presented with contingencies for a lease-up and felt the "nudge" to pursue a different career path in retail.

Do you have an industry specialty or niche?

My specialty is project leasing – power centers, grocery-anchored centers and malls.

What advice do you have for someone entering the commercial real estate industry?

Target an area that you enjoy. Do not feel that you need to be an expert in all fields of real estate.

Did/do you have a mentor and how did you find him or her?

My dad has always been my north star in life and business. Additionally, I have been exposed to industry greats including Henry S. Miller, Ken Hughes and Herb Weitzman.

What is the best advice you have received?

A couple points come to mind - If you are asked a question and do not know the answer, simply state you will find out and respond back. Second, make the tough call first. Deal with the challenging situation as you start your day. Do not procrastinate.

What are three skills you need to be in the industry?

Be politely persistent, have a strong work ethic and be organized. Develop a system for your area of expertise to enhance your market knowledge. Adapt and be willing to change – never use the phrase "this is the way we used to do it."

What failure stands out for you and what did you learn?

While leasing a high-profile center in Dallas, I was officing at our on-site marketing center. One day a reporter stops by someone I knew, and we start visiting. Little did I know, our conversation regarding a potential anchor would later appear on the front page of the Dallas Times Herald Business section. Control the delivery of a message was definitely a lesson learned from this experience!

What are the steps you have taken to succeed in commercial real estate?

I am fortunate to have had an incredibly supportive husband and family. They have encouraged me in so many ways it is hard to quantify. Be willing to work long hours, focus, be flexible, continue to educate yourself and never stop learning. When you are too tired to make that last call of the day, make it! In my case, that last call led to a very important Louis Vuitton deal in 1981.

What question are you asked the most?

Ha! "How much longer do I plan on working!" No boundaries in this career!

What are the greatest challenges you have faced in the industry?

To be taken seriously. There were so very few women in the business when I started, it was easy to be underestimated. I had to stretch myself – develop confidence and believe I could build a career. We are our own worst critics, and this has been a very personal journey for me as well as professionally.

What is the best negotiation tip you have learned?

Listen. Do not feel like you always need to speak. We enhance our position by engaging with the other party.

What time management tools or skills do you use?

Make a list each day of tasks/calls. We get pulled many directions. Prioritize time-sensitive items.

What advice would you give to the next generation of female leaders?

Select a group(s) – not too many – with other industry professionals and network. Support friends are mandatory!

What organizations or groups do you recommend becoming part of your network?

My feeling is the NexGen ICSC groups are great. Also, NTCAR has a variety of programs for many areas specific to your need.

Looking back, what is one thing you wish you knew at the beginning of your career?

Why did I not take that 4th level of accounting in college!

BIO - Lynn Van Amburgh

Lynn Van Amburgh, vice president with Texas-based retail-focused real estate firm Weitzman, is one of Dallas-Fort Worth's most experienced project leasing professionals for regional retail projects. Lynn entered the commercial real estate profession in 1980 with Henry S. Miller Co., where notable properties she represented included Highland Park Village and the pre-leasing for landmark properties The Crescent in Uptown Dallas and Dallas Galleria in Far North Dallas. Lynn's extensive leasing experience with firms including The Nasher Company, General Growth and Simon Property Group included responsibilities for leasing at D-FW-area destinations like NorthPark Center, Stonebriar Centre, The Parks at Arlington and others.

Lynn brought her extensive experience of the needs and requirements for regional-draw projects and retailers alike to Weitzman in 2019. At Weitzman, she handles project representation duties for high-profile centers like Denton's Golden Triangle Mall, Grapevine Towne Center, Firewheel Market and others.

Lynn is an active member of the International Council of Shopping Centers, member of Deals In Heels and Kappa Alpha Theta Dallas Alumnae.

Lynn, a native of Dallas, graduated from Highland Park High School and attended the University of Alabama in Tuscaloosa, Alabama, where she received a Bachelor of Science degree in Business Education.

LISA WALKER

Company: McDonald's

Years in Commercial Real Estate: 31

How did you get started in commercial real estate and what age?

During high school and college, I was involved in dance drill team and worked for the National Cheerleaders Association (NCA) during summers and holidays. After obtaining my undergraduate degree, I continued to work for NCA providing dance instruction and facilitating events across the country. This was a fun out-of-college job, but the pay and upward mobility was limited.

A year later, I found out about a leadership role at a national retailer—Sally Beauty Company—located in Denton Texas, where I lived at the time. The role happened to be in development, where I was overseeing the property and asset management staff. I was told that my background of leading peers and young women was a good fit for this mid-management role. In addition to the supervision of the team, a substantial portion of the role was re-negotiating existing leases with an attempt to reduce the rent and to soften other provisions within our existing leases. I enjoyed this very much and found success in my negotiations while developing relationships with landlords and shopping center personnel across the country. But during this year, I overheard the dealmakers in the cubicles around me having even more success while seeing the country when they traveled to secure new sites. So, I begged to join the dealmaking team when a spot opened. I have stayed on the tenant side of dealmaking and leading dealmaking teams ever since.

Do you have an industry specialty or niche?

After Sally Beauty and Bill's Dollar Store (a now defunct small town general merchandiser) I left to do deals in the restaurant industry at brands like Wendy's, Which Wich, Corner Bakery and El Pollo Loco prior to joining the McDonald's team.

Being on the tenant side of the deal has provided me with stability, a steady paycheck, and other favorable benefits. Tenants, of course, are heavily pursued by developers and brokers; they want us in their shopping centers, and they want the monthly rent we pay! And I have always liked having the leverage of walking away from the transaction if I could not get the terms my brand had to have. It is rewarding to see a deal to fruition, and it is nice to be the bell of the development ball!

And being in the restaurant segment of the tenant side provides additional security in the current Amazon and virtual sales world we live in. Even in a ghost kitchen scenario, there is real estate involved.

Leading deal making teams, which I have done at several brands, is satisfying, and challenging in many other ways. To me it has always been comparable to parenthood, with the highest highs and the lowest lows. Keeping the team motivated, appreciated, and valued is hard work and requires a different skill set when dealing with a variety of personalities.

What advice do you have for someone entering the commercial real estate industry?

First, stick with it! There are many brands and many roles so when you have a bad experience at one place or with one boss, find another role. What that say is true, "when you love what you do, it never feels like work." For 31 years I have never dreaded going to work. I have disliked some of the people I have interacted with, but I have always loved the work.

Second, find your niche. Look for ways to differentiate yourself from the other dealmakers. This can be done easily with some simple business practices. For example: following up after a call or meeting; remembering their spouse and children's names and hobbies; answering the phone or returning calls within 24 hours. These small considerations strengthen your relationship with the landlord. Use your daily actions to be the easiest and most pleasant tenant they deal with so that they think of you for their next great site.

Third, never burn a bridge. The development industry in any given market is small. We all move onto the next deal even when the last one did not go smoothly. Every day you should interact with integrity and humility and show some grace even when others do not.

Did/do you have a mentor and how did you find him or her?

Mentorship has been a big part of my life since the early days of dance drill team. New rookie dancers are teamed with a veteran to learn the ropes and have a safe place to ask questions. It is the same at great brands with dealmaking teams. A lot of brands have a "year one" mentoring program where you are assigned an on-boarding buddy to help guide you through the processes and tools. Take advantage of this and keep in touch long after year one is over. Mentoring is always a great opportunity to meet folks outside of your immediate team and learn cross functional responsibilities.

I have also had several opportunities to mentor young folks entering the development industry through the ICSC mentorship program. I find that I learn as much from them as they do from me. It is rewarding to track these young folks and watch their careers evolve.

What is the best advice you have received?

Steve Farrar, the former COO of The Wendy's Company told me "The cream always rises to the top." In the corporate world you need to deliver results while you continue to develop your skill set for the next role. Have patience if the promotional timeline does not align with where you want your career to be. Enjoy the season of skill-building.

What are three skills you need to be in the industry?

- ➢ Dealmaking is about sourcing the right site and negotiating approvable deal terms

- ➢ To source the right site, you need to be strategic, be connected in the industry, and have creative problem-solving skills

- ➢ To secure approvable deal terms you need to be organized, well spoken, empathetic and credible

What failure stands out for you and what did you learn?

Due to economic environments and brands that have had cyclical success, I have had to change companies unexpectedly and at unfavorable times.

Try to embrace this season as a true learning experience. Enjoy the self-discovery that comes from understanding various roles and evaluating how it would feel to work at that brand. Treat every interview as a networking session regardless of the outcome. Recognize that if you cannot reach your goals at one brand, find another that will satisfy your professional need to contribute in a valuable way.

What are the steps you have taken to succeed in commercial real estate?

I have paid my dues. I have done lesser roles for which I was over-qualified. I have worked for folks with whom I would surely not spend my spare time. I have had to look for the silver lining many times – but it is always there.

I have remained flexible. The truth is that some brands will fail when they try and expand across the country and superior real estate cannot fix it. Even choosing your career path wisely could still yield a short stint at the brand of your dreams. Wise Japanese women know that "You fall down seven times and stand up eight." Stand up and try again. And do not let it define you.

I have used my time wisely. Good deal makers know which sites are approvable. Great deal makers know which of the approvable sites are really going to happen.

I drive for results. I keep my goals directly in front of me every day – staring me in the face. I want to start and end each workday knowing where I stand in delivering those goals. Effort without results is never going to get a new unit open or sell any burgers. Anybody can work long hours, use your hours to effect lasting results.

What question are you asked the most?

Why did not you go to the other side of the deal and be a developer making 3-4 times more money? Because I like the tenant side. I like being the bell of the ball. I like negotiating with tough landlords on behalf of my brand. I like the security and stability that the tenant side of the transaction provides. I like training new team members on how to be efficient and successful with our tools. I like leading a team of high producing deal makers that deliver results and make me proud.

And I ABSOLUTELY LOVE driving by or dining in the new restaurant that exists because I found the real estate and made the deal happen. It is not unusual for me to detour across a city to see a restaurant that I did decades ago when I happen to be back in a place I do not get to often. That restaurant has added incremental sales to the brand. It is tax revenue for the city. It is jobs that continue through generations. It is billions served. But it is also part of the legacy of my career and for me this is rewarding in an incomparable way.

What are the greatest challenges you have faced in the industry?

Economic downturns. Layoffs. Restructuring. Adapting to new leadership. We have all faced these challenges and it can be tough. My advice: Keep your head up. Deliver results. Mentally prepare for change – it is inevitable. The deal makers that can acclimate to change by delivering results in adverse conditions will lead the next team.

What is one tip you learned on how to negotiate?

Understand the value of the deal terms you are bringing to the table. A strong cap rate. A longer termed lease. A consistently maintained and modernized facility. Tremendous traffic to the intersection. A well-run operation.

Then find out exactly what the other side wants and *why*. Recognize that in some cases you can soften your stance on one aspect of the deal to accommodate what the other side needs.

What time management tools or skills do you use?

I keep my calendar completely up to date and in front of me at all times on a separate monitor. I have found that anything can be tackled if it is broken into measurable steps. I like to place quarterly, monthly and weekly 'to do' tasks within my calendar and when applicable invite my team to the event as well to remind them of the task. This has worked well.

What advice would you give to the next generation of female leaders?

Give yourself a break sometimes. You cannot fill anyone else's cup when yours is empty. Let yourself be celebrated when it is deserved. Women are so great at recognizing others but sometimes we need to let ourselves be recognized as the superstar that we are when it is deserved and with an abundance of humility.

Lose the drama. Nobody wins when inappropriate emotion flares. Count to ten, let it go to voicemail or save it as a draft when you know you may not be as professional as the situation calls for. Let the emotion pass and readdress it professionally after you have had time to process the situation.

What organizations or groups do you recommend becoming part of your network?

ICSC nationally and a local real estate group – if you cannot find one, start one.

Looking back, what is one thing you wish you knew at the beginning of your career?

Working smarter is better than working hard. Sometimes the ones at their desk the longest are prolonging the issue by waiting around for input instead of solving the issue themselves.

When a Seller brings you a potential site, the second-best answer you can give them is a fast "no." Do not put off making tough decisions. It is one thing to weigh the options with a business case in hand, but it is another to wait until only one of those options remain. Time does not kill deals, procrastination does. Evaluate the site quickly and communicate truthfully where the deal stands.

BIO - LISA WALKER

Lisa Walker has over 30 years of corporate restaurant real estate experience. She joined the National real estate team at McDonald's in 2019 working multiple markets and for the last two years she has led a portion of the US deal making team.

Prior to McDonald's she led the real estate teams for El Pollo Loco and Wendy's Hamburgers and has handled multiple markets across the nation during critical growth years for Corner Bakery Cafe and Which Wich Sandwiches.

She holds a BS in Organizational Communications from the University of Texas and is a former member of the original dance drill team, the Kilgore College Rangerettes, where she recently served as president of the Rangerettes Forever alumni board. She is a former volunteer of the year for the Women's Foodservice Forum and an active member of a professional DFW women's real estate group called Deals in Heels. She is a published author, podcast subject, and frequent contributor to real estate alumni classrooms at the collegiate level.

When she's not busy sourcing great real estate she can be found spending time with her son and daughter-in-law, reading classic and modern books, country western dancing, and planning international travel with her shopping buddies.

LinkedIn address: https://www.linkedin.com/in/lisaawalker/

RESOURCES

Bisnow www.bisnow.com

CCIM (Certified Commercial Investment Member) www.ccim.com

Chamber of Commerce (local chapter)

Commercial Real Estate Development Association (NAIOP) www.naiop.org

Commercial Real Estate Women (CREW) www.crewnetwork.org

CREW Dallas www.crew-dallas.org

Core Net Global www.corenetglobal.org

Economic Development Centers (EDC) (local city)

Industrial Asset Management Council www.iamc.org

ICSC www.icsc.com

Institute of Real Estate Management (IREM) www.irem.org

International Franchise Association (IFA) www.franchise.org

National Association of Corporate Real Estate Executives (NACORE) www.realestateagent.com

National Multifamily Housing Council (NMHC) www.nmhc.org

North Texas Commercial Association of REALTORS® (NTCAR) www.ntcar.org

Retail Live www.retaillive.com

Rotary Club www.rotary.org

Society of Industrial and Office Realtors (SIOR) www.sior.com

The Real Estate Council (TREC) www.recouncil.com

Urban Land Institute (ULI) www.uli.org

Women In Real Estate (WIRE) www.wirewomeninrealestate.com

Women's Leadership Institute (WLI) www.wliut.com

Made in the USA
Coppell, TX
01 August 2023

19845775R00098